SeinLanguage

ized by Google
JERRY SEINFELD
SeinLanguage

BANTAM BOOKS

New York   Toronto   London   Sydney   Auckland

SeinLanguage

A Bantam Book / September 1993

All rights reserved.
Copyright © 1993 by Jerry Seinfeld
Interior photographs copyright © 1993 by Annie Leibovitz
Book design by Glen M. Edelstein
No part of this book may be reproduced or transmitted in any form or by any means, electronic or mechanical, including photocopying, recording, or by any information storage and retrieval system, without permission in writing from the publisher.
For information address: Bantam Books.

Library of Congress Cataloging-in-Publication Data
Seinfeld, Jerry.
    SeinLanguage / Jerry Seinfeld.
       p. cm.
    ISBN 0-553-09606-0
    I. Title.
PN6162.S358   1993
814'.54—dc20   93-14467
                                                                                     CIP

Published simultaneously in the United States and Canada

Bantam Books are published by Bantam Books, a division of Bantam Doubleday Dell Publishing Group, Inc. Its trademark, consisting of the words "Bantam Books" and the portrayal of a rooster, is Registered in U.S. Patent and Trademark Office and in other countries. Marca Registrada. Bantam Books, 1540 Broadway, New York, New York 10036.

PRINTED IN THE UNITED STATES OF AMERICA
BVG   0 9

CONTENTS

INTRODUCTION	1
FREEWAY OF LOVE	5
PERSONAL MAINTENANCE	27
PALDOM	49
SHUT UP AND DRIVE	65
JOB SECURITY	83
THE THING IS THE THING	101
OUT AND BACK	123
THE RIDE OF YOUR LIFE	151

To my wonderful parents Betty and Kal, and my also wonderful sister Carolyn, who when they heard I wanted to become a comedian, thought it was a great idea.

When I was a kid my father used to take me around with him in his truck. He was in the sign business on Long Island and he had a little shop called the Kal Signfeld Sign Co.

He really did.

I'd ride in the van with my sneakers up on the dashboard and it was there that I first learned one of life's great pleasures, watching other people work.

In truth, there were few people as much fun to watch work as my father. There has never been a professional comedian with better stage presence, attitude, timing, or delivery. He was a comic genius selling painted plastic signs that said things like "Phil's Color TV" and cardboard ones like "If you want to raise cattle, why do you keep shooting the bull?"

The thing I remember most about those afternoons is how often my father would say to me, "Sometimes I don't even care if I get the order, I just have to break that face." He hated to see those serious businessman faces. I guess that's why he, like me, never seemed to be able to hold down any kind of real job.

Often when I'm on stage I'll catch myself imitating a little physical move or certain kind of timing that he would do.

"To break that face."

It was a valued thing in my house. I remember when Alan King would walk out on the *Ed Sullivan Show* hearing my mother say, "Now, quiet." We could talk during the news but not during Alan King. This was an important man.

And I was proud to be the only kid in my neighborhood with a complete Bill Cosby album collection. He was my favorite comedian and the first black actor to star in a series. But to me, he was the first adult on TV to wear sneakers on a regular basis. I know that affected me, but I'm not sure in what way.

My father lived to see me start to make it as a comedian and he was always my most enthusiastic supporter. He taught me a gift is to be given. And just as he gave it to me, I hope I am able to give it to you.

INTRODUCTION

I certainly never imagined at fifteen, when I started writing down these funny thoughts that kept coming into my head, that someday they would amount to a book. I never thought they would amount to anything, really. But a lot of people have this little corner of their brain that wants to play all the time. The idea of this book for me and for you is to keep that corner alive. It's good to play, and you must keep in practice.

I still can't believe this book is in a bookstore. I love bookstores. A bookstore is one of the only pieces of physical evidence we have that people are still thinking. And I like the way it breaks down into fiction and nonfiction. In other words, these people are lying, and these people are telling the truth. That's the way the world should be.

"Hi, I'm Jerry Seinfeld. I'm fiction."

"I know."

"How did you know?"

"Because I'm nonfiction."

I also find a bookstore to be a wonderful laxative. I don't know what it is. I don't know whether it's the quiet, or all the available reading material, but you walk in there and something just happens. I really think they should eliminate a couple of aisles and put in some nice men's and ladies' rooms in the back, and then a bookstore would really be a wonderful place to visit.

I think the biggest problem bookstores have is not enough room by the cash register to sell stuff. They seem to feel this is the only really good selling area. They think "The only way we're going to unload this one is if their money's already out." Why not give each salesperson in the store their own cash register, and let them follow the customers around? When they see someone pick up a book, they sneak up behind them and go, "cha-ching" and the customer will turn around and go, "Well I guess as long as you've got it rung up already . . ."

I would say the main competition for the book is the video because for some reason people feel they need to come home with a rectangular block of something that they don't know the end of. The big advantage of a book is it's very easy to rewind. Close it and you're right back at the beginning.

It must be frustrating to work at a bookstore. They see someone come in, spend two hours, and walk out with nothing. They must want to explode—just push the customer in the back as they exit, "So you know everything? There's nothing you need in here? There must be something you're at least interested in. Why did you come in here in the first place? We don't need you, you know."

In a lot of ways, that's what a bookstore is. It's a "smarter than you" store. And that's why people are intimidated—because to walk into a bookstore, you have to admit there's something you don't know.

And the worst part is you don't even know where it is. You go in the bookstore and you have to ask people, "Where is this? Where is that? Not only do I lack knowledge, I don't even know where to get it." So just to walk into a bookstore you're admitting to the world, "I'm not too bright."

It's pretty impressive, really.

But the pressure is on you now. This book is filled with funny ideas but you have to provide the delivery. So when you read it, remember—timing, inflection, attitude. That's comedy. I've done my part. The performance is up to you.

And if you find at some point that you're not laughing, keep smiling, wipe your brow, and try to get them on the next bit.

FREEWAY OF LOVE

Well that's it, I give up. I really don't know what the women are thinking. I've talked with them. I've studied them. I've asked them to study me. And I have to admit I am still at square one. Not that I really object to square one. It is the only numbered square in the game. At least you know your position. Nobody ever screws up and goes, "Well, back to oval seven."

I believe we're all secretly happy we can't figure our relationships out. It keeps our minds working. I think we have to be grateful for the one thing in our lives that keeps us from being totally focused on eating.

THE DATE

Dating is pressure and tension. What is a date really, but a job interview that lasts all night? The only difference between a date and a job interview is that in not many job interviews is there a chance you'll wind up naked at the end of it.

"Well Bill, the boss thinks you're the man for the position. Why don't you strip down and meet some of the people you'll be working with?"

Maybe we need some kind of pre-date ritual. Maybe first meet up in one of those rooms where you visit prisoners. You have that glass between you. You talk on the phones. See how that goes before you attempt an actual date. This way the only sexual tension would be deciding if you should put your hand on the glass or not. And if you're not comfortable at any point, you just signal to the guard and they take the other person away.

It's hard to have fun when you're feeling evaluated. We should say, "You seem nice. Why don't we get together sometime for some serious scrutiny?"

Because that's the thing that happens. Whenever you think about this person in terms of maybe spending your future with them, you have to magnify every little thing about them.

The guy will be like, "I don't think her eyebrows are even. I can't believe it. Her eyebrows *are* uneven. Could I look at uneven eyebrows for the rest of my life?" And of course, the woman's thinking, "What is he looking at? Do I want someone looking at me like this for the rest of my life?"

Women, of course, have powers far beyond those of mortal men.

A woman left a message on my phone machine the other day, with kind of a breathy voice. And no matter what a woman says, if it's in that breathy voice, it sounds so appealing. A stewardess could lean over, whisper in my ear, "Would you put on your seatbelt? We're about to crash into a mountain." And I would go, "Really? So what are you doing later by the ruptured fuselage? What do you say we meet for some peanuts over by the black box? I'll bring the cushions."

Women need to like the job of the guy they're dating. If they don't like the job, they don't like the guy. Men know this—which is why we make up the phony, bogus names for the jobs that we have. "Well right now, I'm the regional management supervisor. I'm in development, production, consulting . . ."

Men, on the other hand, if they are physically attracted to a woman, are not that concerned with her job.

We'll just go, "Really? Slaughterhouse? Is that where you work? That sounds interesting. So, what do you have, a big cleaver and you just lop their heads right off? That sounds great. Listen, why don't you shower up and we'll get some burgers and catch a movie."

And why is it always dinner? You pick your teeth, I'll wipe my chin, we'll find out what we're really about here. He's thinking, "Boy, nice hair." She's thinking, "I can't believe the size of the piece of bread he just put in his mouth." That always happens to me. Why is it when I reach for the bread I suddenly forget I'm on a date? I have this split-second mental lapse and think I'm alone in a hotel room in Milwaukee. And there's nothing you can do once that bread is in there. You just get it down and hope she likes your car.

What would the world be like if people said whatever they were thinking, all the time, whenever it came to them? How long would a blind date last? About thirteen seconds, I think. "Oh sorry, your rear end is too big." "That's okay, your breath stinks anyway. See you later." "No problem." "Goodbye." "Okay." "Thank you very much."

Dating in modern times is actually a big improvement on past civilizations. You know that in ancient tribal cultures, they would sacrifice a virgin. This is true. They thought that would accomplish something. They would find some girl that had never been out with anybody and they would throw her into a volcano. Now *there's* a first date she'll never forget. She winds up in Heaven, talking with Chuck Woolery. "So, tell me, Lisa, how did the date end?"

"Not well, Chuck. Not well."

"Well, if you'd like to be thrown into a volcano again, we'll pay for it. . . ."

The worst dates are often the result of the fix-up. Why do we fix people up? Because *you* think they'll have a good time? Who the hell are you? It's a little power trip isn't it? You're playing God.

Of course God was the first person to fix people up. Fixed up Adam and Eve, you know. I'm sure he said to Adam, "No, she's nice, she's very free about her body, doesn't really wear much. She was going out with a snake —I think that's over though."

To me, the fix-up just doesn't work. You cannot fix people up. It doesn't work because nobody wants to think that they need to be fixed up. You cannot get that out of your mind; it affects your attitude when you meet the person that you're fixed up with. You go, "Well, I guess everybody thinks I should be with you."

I was fixed up one time. Couldn't deal with it. The whole time we were out, I could feel the puppet strings of the fixer-uppers on me. I couldn't even operate my body. I go to put my arm around her . . .

JERRY SEINFELD

—SLAP—

"Sorry, I can't control my arms. This whole evening wasn't my idea. I'm just a puppet."

Has it ever occurred to you that the ventriloquist dummy always seems to have a very active, sexual, social life? He's always talking about dates and women that he knows and bringing them back to the suitcase at night. There's always a sawdust joke in there somewhere, kinky sexual references to being made out of wood or spinning his head around. We're somehow expected to accept this. I guess because the face is so animated, they think we're not noticing, for example, that the feet are just kind of swinging there. Dummy feet never look really right, do they? Plastic shoes just kind of dangling there. Always kind of askew. You always just see a little ankle, those little thin white fabric ankles that they have. And the thought creeps in: "You know, I think they're trying to put something over on me here."

I've always wanted to invite a woman up to my apartment for a nightcap then just give her one of those little hats that flops over on the side. "That's all. I just wanted to give you that. You can go now. If you want to go out next week, I'll give you a short robe that matches."

Now if you do spend the night at somebody else's house . . . Which happens. It could happen. It's happened to a lot of people. . . . You always think to yourself, "I can handle this. It's no big deal." But your hair the next morning is the true reflection of how you really feel inside. Your hair freaks out when it wakes up at somebody else's house. You go in the bathroom, it's like, "This is not our sink, this is not our brush, this is not our mirror—Aaaah!"

You have to keep it from panicking. "Would you just calm down! We'll be home in a minute."

What can you do at the end of a date when you know you don't want to see this person ever again, for the rest of your life? What do you say? No matter what you say, it's a lie. "I'll see you around?" See you around? Where is that? "If you're around, and I'm around, I'll see you around that area. You'll be around other people, though. You won't be around me. But you will be around."

"Take care now." Did you ever say that to somebody?

"Take care now. Take care, *now*. Because I'm not going to be taking care of you. So you should take care of yourself now."

"Take care, take care." What does this mean, "Take care?"

"Take off." Isn't that what you really want to say? "Take off now. Get out of here."

THE SEX

The problem with the sex-orientation process is that every person has their own sexual timetable of what should happen when. The other person of course knows nothing about it, and no one's talking. We all have this demeanor like that poster of W. C. Fields in the poker game.

That's why I think we need some sort of sexual rulebook where it's written down and agreed upon, a sexual standard dating procedure. If there are any problems, you simply refer to it and go, "Look honey, I'm very sorry, but we've been out three times and according to Article 7, Section 5, there's got to be some physical contact, as you can see right there. Otherwise I will report you to the board and they can put out a warrant for an embrace."

And a woman can go, "First of all, if you think meeting me for a half hour on my lunch break for a small yogurt, no topping, is going to hold up as a date in front of that board you can forget it. Not to mention calling me 'honey' before the end of the three-week endearment moratorium period. That's a misdemeanor, you know."

Seems to me the basic conflict between men and women, sexually, is that men are like firemen. To us, sex is an emergency, and no matter what we're doing we can be ready in two minutes. Women, on the other hand, are like fire. They're very exciting, but the conditions have to be exactly right for it to occur.

Men and women, all in all, behave just like our basic sexual elements. If you watch single men on a weekend night they really act very much like sperm—all disorganized, bumping into their friends, swimming in the wrong direction.

"I was first."

"Let me through."

"You're on my tail."

"That's my spot."

We're like the Three Billion Stooges.

But the egg is very cool: "Well, who's it going to be? I can divide. I can wait a month. I'm not swimming anywhere."

Which brings us to the condom. There's nothing wrong with the condom itself. The problem with condoms is still buying them. I think we should have like a secret signal with the druggist. You just walk into the drugstore, you go up to the counter, he looks at you and if you nod slowly, he puts them in the bag for you. That's it.

You show up there, you put your little shaving cream, your little toothpaste on the counter.

"How are you today?" (You nod.)

"Not bad. Yourself?" (He puts them in.)

"Oh, pretty good."

And you've got them.

Nakedness is a big thing with men. We're living for the naked city. Whatever it is that you won't show us, that's what we're obsessed with seeing. I mean, if women always wore hats in public all the time, you'd see men buying *Playhead* magazine. Reading "Skulls of the Big Ten." This would be our only interest.

You start wondering about these cultures in *National Geographic* where everybody's naked, you know? You see all these people and you wonder, "What are the men in these cultures trying to look at when women walk by?" Could you have a strip club in a place like that? Woman goes on stage, takes off the necklace, takes out the nose ring—that's it, show's over. Men are in the audience going, "Wow, you see that little indentation there in the top of her lip? I told you, man. This place is hot!"

That's why fashion works on men. Every year women cover up one thing, show us something else. Drives us wild. We never catch on that you've been alternately concealing and revealing the exact same things to us for centuries. We don't know.

Every time women put on a new outfit we're mystified all over again. "I think the boobs are in there."

"Really? I think they're over there."

What about talking during sex? The question is: Does the talking really improve the sex, or is the sex act there now just to spice up the conversation?

Of course, eventually, I'm sure people will get tired or too lazy even for phone sex. They'll start having phone-machine sex. They'll be really bored, "Yeah, I want you really bad. Just leave it on the tape."

Then I guess the phone company will come out with sex waiting. That'll be the new thing. "Uh, yeah, hold on honey it's the other line. . . . Oh, hiya baby. One second. . . . Uh, honey, I've gotta take this. Yeah, I've got sex waiting on the other line. I've *got* to take this call."

THE RELATIONSHIP

See, each man and each woman actually does have an owner's manual. Nothing's written down anywhere, but the directions for operation of an individual in a relationship are detailed and specific nonetheless. So when you start out with someone, you're essentially driving a strange car for the first time and none of the controls are labeled. So the wipers can come on at strange times, sometimes you stall. On top of that we've all met people with bad steering, no brakes, needs a muffler, headlights a little dim, too much in the trunk, not enough under the hood, prone to backfiring, won't turn over, and just plain out of gas. Which is why when people get ready to get married they so often seem to choose basic transportation. It's simple, it's reliable, and it gets you there. That's important on a long trip.

What is the problem, why is commitment such a big problem for a man? I think that for some reason when a man is driving down that freeway of love, the woman he's involved with is like an exit, but he doesn't want to get off there. He wants to keep driving. And the woman is like, "Look, gas, food, lodging, that's our exit, that's everything we need to be happy . . . Get off here, now!" But the man is focusing on the sign underneath that says, "Next exit twenty-seven miles," and he thinks, "I can make it." Sometimes he can, sometimes he can't. Sometimes the car ends up on the side of the road with the hood up and smoke pouring out of the engine. He's sitting on the curb all alone, "I guess I didn't realize how many miles I was racking up."

JERRY SEINFELD

For me, the best part of a relationship is when you're sick. And the best time to be sick is in a relationship.

If I have to get married, you know all those vows, "For richer or for poorer, for better or for worse . . ."

All I need is the sickness part. That to me is the most important one. "Do you take this man in sickness?" The rest of the time go out, have a ball, do whatever you want —but if I get the sniffles, you'd better be there.

Don't get me wrong, the wedding ceremony is a beautiful thing. The vows, the costumes. I think the idea behind the tuxedo is the woman's point of view that "Men are all the same, we might as well dress them that way."

That's why, to me, a wedding is like the joining together of a beautiful, glowing bride, and some guy. The tuxedo is a wedding safety device, created by women, because they know that men are undependable. So in case the groom chickens out, everybody just takes one step over, and she marries the next guy.

That's why the wedding vow isn't, "Do you take Bill Simpson?"

It's, "Do you take this man?"

I have a friend who's about to get married. They're having the bachelor party and the bridal shower the same day. So it's conceivable that while the girl's friends are giving her sexy lingerie, the guy could be at a nude bar watching a table dancer in the exact same outfit. I think that'll be a very special moment.

To me, the difference between being single and married is the form of government. When you're single, you are the dictator of your own life. You have complete power. When I give the order to fall asleep on the sofa with the TV on in the middle of the day, no one can overrule me! When you're married, you are part of a vast decision-making body. Before anything is accomplished, there's got to be meetings, committees have to study the situation.

And this is if the marriage works. I think this is the reason why divorce is so painful. You've been impeached and you weren't even the President.

THE END

There's no easy way to break off any relationship.

It's like the mozzarella cheese on a good slice of pizza. No matter how far you pull the slice away from your mouth it just gets thinner and longer but never snaps. Of course you could always just eat your pizza with a knife and fork, but I think this is clearly what's known as "pushing the cheese analogy."

One way to end the relationship is adultery. Adultery. Now that's a heavy thing. You can't just have an adultery, you must commit adultery. But you can't commit adultery unless you have a commitment. So you have to make the commitment before you can even think about committing it. There's no commit without the commit. Once you commit, then you can commit the adultery, then you can get caught, get divorced, lose your mind, and they have you committed.

But you know, some people actually cheat on the

people that they're cheating with, which is like holding up a bank and then turning to the robber next to you and going, "All right, give me everything you got, too."

I think that even if you've had a relationship with someone—or let's say, *especially* if you've had a relationship with someone—and you try to become friends afterward, it's very difficult.

Because you know each other so well. You know all each other's tricks. It's like two magicians trying to entertain each other.

The one goes, "Look, a rabbit."

The other goes, "So? . . . I believe this is your card."

"Look, why don't we just saw each other in half and call it a night? Okay?"

I think when you first start dating, they ought to give you three "Get Out of Relationship Free" cards so you can just go up to the person and say, "Uh, here you go. I'm sorry. I'll grab my tennis racket. Don't get up. Best of luck. Sorry."

Which is fine—unless, of course, the person you're in the relationship with happens to have an "Eight More Months of Guilt, Torture, and Pain" card.

"Uh, hold it, I think I've got a little something for you. . . ."

PERSONAL MAINTENANCE

Let's face it, the human body is like a condominium apartment. The thing that keeps you from really enjoying it is the maintenance. There's a tremendous amount of daily, weekly, monthly, and yearly work that has to be done. From showering to open heart surgery, we're always doing something to ourselves. If your body was a used car, you wouldn't buy it. You'd go, "Nah, I've heard about these human being bodies. This is one of those Earth models, right? Yeah, a cousin of mine had one. Too much work to keep them going. The new ones are nice looking, though."

THE UPKEEP

Women definitely go to maintenance extremes. It's amazing the way women take care of all the hair on their bodies. One of the great mysteries to me is the fact that a woman could pour hot wax on her legs, rip the hair out by the roots, and still be afraid of a spider.

Sometimes they go even further than that—electrolysis. That's giving your hair the chair. It's the death penalty for hair. You put him in a little chair, you put the little metal cap on him, give him his last shampoo, whatever creme rinse he wants. The only thing that can save him is a call from the Epilady.

For men, the transplant is the hair procedure of choice. The hair plug is an interesting process. It's really quite amazing. Hair that was on your shower soap yesterday can be in your head tomorrow.

How did they do the first transplant? Did they have the guy take a shower, get his soap, rush it in to the hospital by helicopter, keep the soap alive on a

JERRY SEINFELD

soap-support system? Eventually they move it over, "We got the hairs, but . . . I think we lost the Zest."

Sometimes a body rejects a vital-organ transplant. Is it possible that a head could reject a hair transplant? The guy's just standing around, suddenly "bink"—it lands in someone's frozen yogurt.

There are many cosmetic-surgery procedures available to people today.

Liposuction, for instance. Are you familiar with this? This is a fat-sucking machine. Now you know that somewhere, somebody is working on a way to make this available in a restaurant. So you could just order it off the menu.

"I'll tell you what, gimme the cheesecake, crank me up to 9, and put a scoop of ice cream on the side."

One of the most popular procedures today is the nose job. The technical term for the nose job is rhinoplasty. Rhino? I mean, do we really need to insult the person at this particular moment of their life? They know they have a big nose, that's why they're coming in. Do they really need the abuse of being compared to a rhinoceros on top of everything else?

When someone goes in for a hair transplant, they don't say, "We're going to perform a cueball-ectomy on you, Mr. Johnson. We're going to attempt to remove the skin-headia of your chrome-domus . . . these are the technical terms, of course."

While I haven't had any cosmetic surgery . . . Does having teeth pulled count? What about shaving? It's cosmetic, there's blood . . . I do have a regular physical examination. Giving them that urine sample, that's always a pleasure isn't it? There's always the amount question. "I don't know what you need. I mean, I gave you whatever I had there. I've got more. I mean, whatever you need I can get it for you. Just let me know what's necessary and I'm sure eventually I can meet the requirement."

With any kind of physical test, I don't know what it is, I always seem to get competitive. Remember when you were in school and they'd do those hearing tests? And you'd really be listening hard, you know?

I wanted to do unbelievable on the hearing test. I

wanted them to come over to me after and go, "We think you may have something close to super-hearing. What you heard was a cotton ball touching a piece of felt. We're sending the results to Washington, we'd like you to meet the President."

We all think we're experts on our own bodies. I was in the drug store the other day trying to get a cold medication. Did you ever try to pick one of these out? Not easy. There's an entire wall of products that you need. You stand there going, "Well, this one is quick acting but this is long lasting. . . . Which is more important, the present or the future?"

I read recently that wine can actually improve your health by reducing the risk of heart attack, hardening of the arteries and cholesterol. This is good news, unless you're a wino. They see this, "Oh no, I'm getting better. That means eight *extra* years of sleeping in doorways wearing 7 hats."

Medical science is actually making advances every day to control health problems. In fact, it's probably only a matter of time before a heart attack becomes like a headache. We'll someday see people on TV saying, "I had a heart attack this big, but I gave myself one of these."

He puts the electro-paddles on his chest.

"Clear!"

Baroom!

". . . and it's gone."

Smoking is certainly one of the oddest and stupidest human idiosyncrasies. Why did anyone think a camel is a good product image for a cigarette? I think each one is the equivalent tar of smoking an actual Camel.

I love the ad campaign they had a few years ago on their anniversary, "75 years and still smoking."

Well, not everybody. I think there might be a few empty chairs at that big birthday bash.

Maybe the appeal is the fire. There's something very scary and exciting about fire. People always run to see a fire. They're very proud that they have a fireplace. This is what smoking is really all about. The power of "I've got some fire right here in my hand. Smoke and fire is literally coming right out of my mouth." And it's very intimidating to the nonsmoker because it's like talking to someone who's going, "My head could open up, lava could explode out, pour right down my face, doesn't bother me a bit." And the cigar is even worse. A cigar is like, "You think this end is scary, look at this wet, disgusting, chewed up nub."

Whatever happened to Raleigh cigarettes? Remember Raleighs? With valuable Raleigh coupons. Real valuable. Each one is worth $1/1000$th of a penny.

You lose a lung trying to get a badminton set. Even if you get it you can't play.

"Cough, cough. Let's smoke a few more packs. I can get a new birdie."

Of course, everyone wants to be healthy. The amusing thing is no one's really sure how to do it.

I love to exercise, but I still have to laugh at it. You go to the health club, you see all these people and they're working out; they're training, they're getting in shape. But nobody's really getting in shape *for* anything. In modern society, you really don't have to be physically strong to do anything. The only reason that you're getting in shape is so you can get through the workout. So we're working out, so that we'll be in shape, for when we have to do our exercises. That's comedy.

I once tried one of these relaxation float tanks. It's this big tank and you get in it with about 500 lbs. of salt dissolved in water so you float.

Now I've found the best thing to do with one of these things is to get in there with a bunch of paper cuts and some razor burn. By the time they let you out, your body will have taken the shape of the inside of that container. Then you won't need a relaxation tank because you'll actually be one.

The other thing I don't get about working out is why we're so careful about locking up our dirty towels, filthy shorts, and smelly jockstraps. What exactly is the black-market value on these disgusting items?

I give my car to any guy in front of a restaurant because he's got a short red jacket— "I guess he's the valet guy." I don't even think about it. But for my hideous, putrefied gym clothes I got one of these locks, you can put a bullet through it and it won't open.

That stuff is safe.

JERRY SEINFELD

Well, I'm getting down to that little sliver of soap in my shower again. I'm going to have to make a decision pretty soon. Throw it out or try to do that Vulcan mind-meld to the next bar. If you do that with every bar, how much free soap does that come out to be at the end of your life? Does it really add up? Do you one day look around and discover you're hundreds of bars ahead of everybody else? You're throwing soap parties. Giving it away around the office.

"Here, Joe. Happy Wednesday."

"Gee, thanks. Where do you get it all?"

"I have my methods."

"Wow, that guy sure has a lot of soap."

"Yeah, he's quite a guy."

Can someone please tell me what is the deal with B.O.? Why do we need B.O.? Everything in nature has a function, a purpose, except B.O.

Doesn't make any sense. Do something good—hard work, exercise—smell very bad. This is the way the human being is designed. You move, you stink.

Why don't our bodies help us? Why can't sweat smell good? Be a different world, wouldn't it? Instead of putting your laundry in the hamper, you'd put it in a vase. Go down to the drugstore, pick up some odorant and perspirant. You'd have a dirty sweatsock hanging from the rearview mirror of your car.

And then on a really special night, maybe a little underwear coming out of your breast pocket, just to show her that she's important.

THE OUTFITS

I think I was named best-dressed man one year. But I don't remember the year and I don't remember what I was wearing. You want to know the truth? (and I can't believe anyone actually has to be asked that) I hate clothes. I hate them, okay?

I hate the selecting, the trying on, the conversing with the sales help. There's another oxymoron, sales-help. You're either helping me or selling me but they're not the same thing. I hate carrying shopping bags. I hate receipts. I hate tags, pins, labels, hangers, buttons, zippers, drawstrings, lapels. I hate bleach, color-safe bleach, detergents, liquids, powders, tablets, stain lifters, stain fighters, stain neutralizers, special crystals, active ingredients, enzymes, whiteners, brighteners. I hate hot water, cold water, warm

JERRY SEINFELD

water. I hate getting $1 off. I hate getting ⅓ more FREE. I hate fabric softener and static cling, so I lose either way. I hate detergents that are good for the environment, bad for the environment, not even aware of the environment. I hate carrying laundry bags. I hate dry cleaning plastic, people that work at dry cleaners, talking about my stains to the dry cleaner. I hate and refuse to read any poster or notice about anything on the wall of the dry cleaner. If it was posted "We reserve the right to steal your clothes," I wouldn't care. I'm not interested. Just take the clothes. Just let me get the hell out of here and back to the world as soon as possible.

Let's get one thing straight about dry cleaning right now. It doesn't exist. There's no such thing as dry cleaning. There's no way of cleaning with dry, washing with dry, or doing anything with dry. Dry itself is nothing. You can't use it. You can't do anything with it. It's not there. Dry is nothing. Are you listening to me? And we walk into these places with the big signs out front, "Dry Cleaning," and somehow never question how they were able to put this absurd concept over on us.

If I gave you a filthy shirt and said, "I want this immaculate. And no liquids!" what are you going to do?

Shake it? Tap it? Blow on it? Give me a break. You almost can't get something dirty with dry, let alone cleaning it.

And "One-Hour Martinizing"? Come on. We inspect, examine, and scrutinize every square inch of our lives yet the whole Martinizing charade just goes completely by us without a word. You know what I think One-Hour Martinizing is? I think they just put the clothes in plastic and give it right back to me. That's One-Hour Martinizing. You can get One-Second Martinizing if you want it.

I once had a leather jacket that got ruined in the rain. Now why does moisture ruin leather? Aren't cows outside a lot of the time?

When it's raining, do cows go up to the farmhouse, "Let us in! We're all wearing leather! Open the door! We're going to ruin the whole outfit here!"

"Is it suede?"

"I *am* suede! The whole thing is suede! I can't have this cleaned. . . . It's all I got!"

I am so tired of having to come up with another little outfit for myself every day. In fact, I will say this—and I think many people agree with me—I think eventually fashion won't even exist. I think someday we'll all wear the same thing. Because anytime I see a movie or a TV show where there are people from the future or another planet, they're all wearing the same outfit. Somehow they all decided, "All right, that's enough. From now on, this is going to be our outfit. One-piece silver jump suit, with a V-stripe on the chest, and boots. That's it. We're going to start visiting other planets and we want to look like a team."

The suit is definitely the universal business outfit for men. There is nothing else that men like to wear when they're doing business. I don't know why it projects this image of power. Why is it intimidating?

"We'd better do what this guy says, his pants match his jacket."

Men love the suit so much, we've actually styled our pajamas to look like a tiny suit. Our pajamas have little lapels, little cuffs, simulated breast pocket. Do you need a breast pocket on your pajamas? You put a pen in there, you roll over in the middle of the night, you kill yourself.

And why the little plastic bag with the extra buttons in the suit-jacket pocket? What kind of a sicko would save these, keep thousands of them in a huge file so he'll always be prepared? "Where the hell is that button?"

Is it that hard to get black, round buttons, that they have to make it into a whole thing? Like you've got such a great jacket, so unique, so one-of-a-kind. "You'll never find buttons like these, we'll save you the trouble of knocking your brains out looking. Because we know they're going to fall off, too." That's the other thing they're trying to tell you.

Even when you die, they bury you in a suit. All the other men stand around. "Boy, it's a shame he died. It's a beautiful suit." The one good thing is that when it's your funeral, you can definitely get same-day alterations, no questions asked.

"This'll be ready next Tuesday."

"Oh, no, we've got to have it by today, this is his last day. I don't think he's going to get another chance to wear it."

JERRY SEINFELD

The proof that we don't understand death is we give dead people a pillow. I mean if you can't stretch out and get some solid rest at that point, I don't think there are any bedding accessories that can make the difference. But the suit and the pillow really shows how we have no idea what to get these people ready for. I mean, what situation are you going into with a suit and a pillow? There's no business nap meetings.

Buying clothes is always tricky. But when there's loud music playing, it really throws your judgment. You look at stuff like, "Hey, if there was a cool party and I was a cool guy, this might be a cool shirt."

You get it home, there's no music, there's no party, and you're not a cool guy.

You're the same chump, 75 bucks lighter.

Women approach clothes from a different angle altogether. The other day I was watching women in a department store looking at clothes, and I noticed women don't try on the clothes, they get behind the clothes. They take a dress off the rack and they hold it up against themselves. They can tell something from this. They stick one leg way out and kind of lean back. I guess they need to know, "If someday I'm one-legged at a forty-five-degree angle, what am I going to wear?"

You never see a man do that. You never see a guy take a suit off the rack, put his head behind the collar, and go, "What do you think about this suit? I think I'll get it. Put some shoes by the bottom of the pants, I want to make sure. Now what if I'm walking? Move the shoes, move the shoes, move the shoes."

I love watching women put on their perfume. They're very careful. They have their little stratego areas. Places they think we're going. They always hit the inside of the wrist. Women are convinced that this is the most action-packed area that could ever happen. Why, ladies? What is happening there? Is that in case you slap the guy? He still finds you intriguing. . . .

—CRACK!—

He turns back, "Oh . . . Chanel."

What is the real idea behind wearing these fragrances? Are we hoping, "Maybe people will think I really smell like this."

JERRY SEINFELD

Someone gave me one of those gift sets. Has the cologne, after-shave, soap-on-a-rope. I need soap on a rope. Lot of times I'm in the shower and I want to hang myself. Why do they connect these two things? Because they rhyme? I don't need shaving cream on a wooden beam.

I even have the underarm deodorant with the cologne smell. Why do you want the smell there? I think once a woman's got her nose in your armpit, the seduction's pretty much over. I think she likes you. Are we like dogs now, where you have to smell every square inch of a person before you make up your mind?

Even dogs just go by looks once in a while.

I think the wonderful thing about men and women is how interested we are in these people we have virtually nothing in common with. Men are obsessed with cleavage, women are obsessed with shoes. It's the exact same obsession. It doesn't matter how many times we've seen these things, every time these objects are presented to us, we have to look. We cannot not look.

To men, cleavage is like the nearest thing to a UFO landing nearby, that's what it is. To women, buying a pair of shoes that they really love is like boarding the alien ship. I think it's entirely possible that aliens have landed and they haven't been able to get our attention because we're so preoccupied with cleavage and shoes.

Why is it so difficult and uncomfortable to be naked? It's because when you have clothes on, you can always make those little adjustments that people love to do. Hitching, straightening, adjusting. You know, you feel like you're getting it together. "Yeah, pretty good. Feeling good, feeling pretty good." But when you're naked, it's so final. You're just, "Well, this is it. There's nothing else I can do."

That's why I like to wear a belt when I'm naked. I feel it gives me something. I'd like to get pockets to hang off the belt. Wouldn't that be the ultimate thing? Picture that. To be naked and still be able to put your hands in your pockets. I think that would really help a lot.

PALDOM

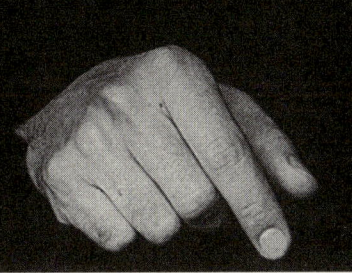

Friends are the DNA of society. They are the basic building blocks of life. If you have a couple of good ones, treasure them like gold. There's nothing better. Ever look at that MCI ad they have, "Friends and Family"?

Who do they mention first?

Your friends help you carry the big weight in life.

That big burden we've all got called,

"What the hell am I doing?"

THE MALE CODE

All plans between men are tentative.

If one man should suddenly have an opportunity to pursue a woman, it's like these two guys never met each other in life. This is the male code.

And it doesn't matter how important the arrangements are. Most of the time they scrub a space-shuttle mission it's because one of the astronauts met someone. He's leaning against the rocket talking to her, "So listen, when I get back, what do you say we get together for some Tang?"

A man is paralyzed mentally by a beautiful woman, and advertisers really take advantage of this. Don't you love those ads where you see the woman in the bikini next to the 32-piece ratchet set? And we'll be looking at the girl in the bikini, then looking at the ratchet set, going, "All right, well if she's right next to the ratchet set, and I *had* that ratchet set . . . I wonder if that would mean that . . . I better just buy the ratchet set."

JERRY SEINFELD

I am not gay, I am however, thin, single, and neat. Sometimes when someone is thin, single, and neat, people assume they are gay because that is the stereotype. You normally don't think of gay people as fat, sloppy, and married. Although I'm sure some are—I don't want to perpetuate a stereotype—but they're probably in the minority within the gay community. They're probably discriminated against because of that. People say to them, "You know Joe, I enjoy being gay with you, but I think it's about time you got in shape, tucked your shirt in and lost the wife."

But if people are going to assume that people who are neat are gay, maybe instead of making that little tilting hand gesture and saying, "You know I think Joe might be a little . . . well, you know . . ." They should mime vacuuming, "You know I think Joe might be a little . . . vrrrrrm."

"Yeah, I had a feeling he was a little vrrrrrm . . ."

What causes homophobia? What is it that makes the heterosexual man worry about this? I think it's because deep down all men know that we have weak sales resistance. We're constantly buying shoes that hurt us, pants that don't fit right. Men think, "Obviously, I can be talked into anything. What if I accidentally wander into some sort of homosexual store thinking it's a shoe store and the salesman says, 'Just hold this guy's hand, walk around a little bit, see how it feels. No obligation, no pressure, just try it.'"

GETTING THE MESSAGE

I've come to the conclusion that there are certain friends in your life who are always your friends and you just have to accept it. You see them even though you don't really want to see them. You don't call them, they call you. You don't call back, they call again. You're late, they wait. You don't show up, they're not upset. You try and stab them, they understand.

The only way to get through talking with people that you don't really have anything in common with is to pretend you're hosting your own little talk show. This is what I do. You pretend there's a little desk around you. There's a little chair over there and you interview them. The only problem with this is there's no way you can say,

JERRY SEINFELD

"Hey, it's been great having you on the show, but I'm afraid we're out of time."

The problem with talking is that nobody stops you from saying the wrong thing. I think life would be a lot better if it was like you're always making a movie. You mess up, somebody just walks on the set and stops the whole shot.

Think of the things you wish you could take back. You're out somewhere with people. "Boy, you look pregnant, are you?" "Cut, cut, cut, cut, that's not going to work at all. Walk out the door, come back in, let's take this whole scene again. People, think about what you're saying."

Have you ever called someone up and you're disappointed when they answer the phone? You wanted the machine. And you're always kind of thrown off. You go, "Oh I uh, I, didn't know you were there, I just wanted to leave a message saying, 'Sorry I missed you.'"

So because of the phone machine, what you can have is two people that don't really ever want to talk, and the phone machine is like this relationship respirator keeping these marginal, brain-dead relationships alive. Why do we do this? Because when we come home we want to see that little flashing red light and go, "All right, messages." People need that. It's very important for human beings to feel they are popular and well-liked amongst a large group of people that they have no interest in.

I love my phone machine. I wish I was a phone machine. I wish if I saw somebody on the street I didn't want to talk to I could just go, "Excuse me, I'm not here right now. If you just leave a message, I can walk away."

I also have a cordless phone, but I don't like that much. Because you can't slam down a cordless phone. You get mad at somebody on a real phone, "You can't talk to me like that!" BANG, it's over. But a cordless phone—"You can't talk to me like that! All right now, let me just find that little thing to turn this off. . . . Just hang on, I'm hanging up on you."

To me, nothing matches the phone machine as a modern technological accomplishment. First of all, look at how long it took before they made ones that actually worked.

Ever take your clock radio or your stereo in to be fixed or returned? Never. They always work perfect. For

JERRY SEINFELD

some reason phone machines are like old Italian cars. You have to take them to obscure little fix-it shops in strange neighborhoods. And when they break, people scoop them up and carry them in their arms like sick children. They yell at befuddled repairmen, "What do you mean there's nothing you can do?"

This is why the phone machine is our most important piece of technology. Look how we care about it. What other machine has such an intimate relationship with you? Who called and when, exactly what they said, how they sounded. Your best friend can't give you such details. Only your phone machine lives and dies with you as you replay the triumphs and disappointments of the day's calls.

It's like your little message fisherman. You come in the door, "How was the catch today? They biting?" I'm sure somewhere someone has returned a phone machine, like a bad lure, because it didn't get enough calls.

I would say the concept behind the car phone, and the phone machine, the speaker phone, the airline phone, the portable phone, the pay phone, the cordless phone, the multi-line phone, the phone pager, the call waiting, the call forwarding, call conferencing, speed dialing, direct dialing, and the redialing, is that we all have absolutely nothing to say, and we've got to talk to someone about it right now. Cannot wait another second!

I mean come on, you're at home you're on the phone, you're in the car you're makin' calls, you get to work, "Any messages for me?" You've got to give people a chance to miss you a little bit.

The downside of the message is it usually means somebody wants something from you. There's two types of favors, the big favor and the small favor. You can measure the size of the favor by the pause that a person takes after they ask you to "Do me a favor." Small favor—small pause. "Can you do me a favor, hand me that pencil." No pause at all. Big favors are, "Could you do me a favor. . . ." Eight seconds go by. "Yeah? What?" ". . . well." The longer it takes them to get to it, the bigger the pain it's going to be.

Humans are the only species that do favors. Animals don't do favors. A lizard doesn't go up to a cockroach and say, "Could you do me a favor and hold still, I'd like to eat you alive." That's a big favor even with no pause.

It's tough to do a good deed. Let's look at your professional good-deed doers, your Lone Rangers, your

Supermen, your Batmen, your Spidermen. They're all wearing disguises, masks over their faces, secret identities. They don't want people to know who they are. Too much aggravation. "Superman, yeah thanks for saving my life, but did you have to come through my wall? I'm renting here. They've got a security deposit. Now what am I supposed to do?"

THE GIFT OF FRIENDSHIP

I am getting a little tired of pretending I'm excited every time it's somebody's birthday. I mean really, at this point, what is the big deal? How many times do we have to celebrate that someone was born? Every year, every person, over and over? All you did was not die for twelve months. This is the big accomplishment?

Nobody likes having "Happy Birthday" sung to them. Nobody likes those icky white frosting cakes. Nobody likes pretending they like the gift.

"Do you really like it?"

"Yes, I do."

"Because if you don't, you can return it and get something else."*

"No, no, I really like it."*

"I want to be sure you like it."*

"Yes, I love it."*

"I had a feeling you'd like it."*

"You know, it's perfect."*

* These are all lies.

There's an entire industry of bad gifts. All those "executive" gifts, any stupid, goofy, brass wood thing, they put a piece of green felt on the bottom, "It's a golf-desk-tie-stress-organizer, Dad."

Nothing compares with the paperweight as a bad gift. To me, there's no better way than a paperweight to express to someone, "I refused to put any thought into this at all." And where are these people working that the papers are just blowing right off of their desks anyway? Is their office screwed to the back of a flatbed truck going down the highway or something? Are they typing up in the crow's nest of a clipper ship? What do you need a paperweight for? Where's the wind coming from?

JERRY SEINFELD

Somebody just gave me a shower radio. Thanks a lot. Do you really want music in the shower? I guess there's no better place to dance than a slick surface next to a glass door.

I also love the gift certificate. That's another real slap in the face, isn't it? It's got that little, bogus border around the edge, so it looks real official. It's an "I-don't-give-a-damn diploma." That's what a gift certificate is.

The clearest indication of the complexity of modern relationships is that greeting card companies are forced to put out cards that are blank on the inside. Nothing . . . no message. It's like the card companies say, "We give up, you think of something. For seventy-five cents it's not worth us getting involved."

And what about the soft-focus people on the cards? You know the ones I mean? They're having a picnic with a tree and a horse and a pond. They're in the canoe and they're paddling along. Is this supposed to remind us of ourselves? Are those people we're supposed to want to be like? I don't know. What would you write inside a card like that anyway? "Here's another couple having a better relationship than *us*. . . . *They* certainly seem to be getting along."

I love those astrology cards where they tell you all the people that have the same birthday as you. It's always an odd group of people too, isn't it? It's like Ed Asner, Elijah Mohammed, and Secretariat. "Yeah, I've always felt I had something in common with them."

My friend just had a baby. There is so much pressure to see this baby. Every time I talk to them, they say, "You have got to see the baby. When are you coming over to see the baby? See the baby. See the baby."

Nobody ever wants you to come over and see their grandfather. "You gotta see him. He's sooo cute. A hundred and sixty-eight pounds, four ounces. I love when they're this age. He's a thousand months. You know the mid-eighties is such a good time for grandpeople. You've got to see him. He went to the bathroom by himself today."

What's tough about seeing people when they have a new baby is that you have to try and match their level of enthusiasm. They're always so excited. "What do you think of him? What do you think?"

Just once I would like to meet a couple that goes, "You know, we're not that happy with him frankly. I think we really made a big mistake. We should've gotten an aquarium. You want him? We've really had enough."

JERRY SEINFELD

Those baby visits can get a lit-tle boring. You have to yawn. It's either yawn or leave. I don't think there's anything wrong with yawning. I hate when people try not to yawn. First of all, we all know you're yawning. Teeth clenched, their cheeks start vibrating, trying to keep their mouth closed. It's like watching someone get electrocuted. Electrocute. There's another word that's kind of strange when you break it down. Electro-cute. What's cute about it? "Would you mind putting on this cute little metal hat for me? This is going to be just the sweetest 50,000 volts you ever felt." Electro-cute. It's like, "Oh no, we're not going to hang you. We're just going to do this little thing we call rope-dee-doo."

SHUT UP AND DRIVE

I love to travel. Much more than I've ever enjoyed getting anywhere. Arrival is overrated. Moving is much more exciting. Planes, boats, cars, trains, feet, whatever. I just want to move. I think destinations were invented just so we all wouldn't look like we were wandering around in a daze.

My all-time favorite form of motion is the car. I'm one of those people. I love cars. It's the greatest physical object I've ever seen. I don't know why, really. My only theory is, when you're driving, you're outside and inside, moving and completely still, all at the same time. I think that's something.

ON THE GROUND

In parking lots now, they have these "Compact Car Only" spots. Isn't that discrimination against the size of your car? If I want my ass hanging out of the back of my parking spot, that's my business. There are people out there with real asses hanging out of their pants, nobody's stopping them. Nobody goes, "Hey, hold it sir, those are compact jeans, you can't pull that in there."

Have you ever been walking down the street and there's a car following you because they think you're going to your car and they want the space? Isn't it weird when a car is going the same speed that you're going? You notice that you stop, they stop, you turn, they turn—it's like having your own giant remote control car. You could break into a sprint, and try to run it into a wall. You can weave back and forth, the guy gets pulled over for drunk driving. It's fun.

JERRY SEINFELD

It seems to me the way they design the car alarm is so that the car will behave as if it were a nervous, hysterical person. Anyone goes near it, anyone disturbs it, it just goes, "Waahaahaahaah!" Lights flashing on and off, acting all crazy. Not everyone wants to draw that much attention to themselves. Wouldn't it be nice if you could have a car alarm that was a little more subtle? Somebody tries to break in the car and it goes, "Uh, ahem. Ahem. Excuse me?" I would like a car alarm like that.

People will kill each other for a parking space in New York because they think, "If I don't get this one, I may never get a space. I'll be searching for months until somebody goes out to the Hamptons." Because everybody in New York City knows there's way more cars than parking spaces. You see cars driving in New York all hours of the night. It's like musical chairs except everybody sat down around 1964.

The problem is, while car manufacturers are building hundreds of thousands of new cars every year, they're not making any new spaces. That's what they should be working on. Wouldn't that be great, you go to the auto show and they've got a big revolving turntable with nothing on it.

"New from Chrysler, a space."

The handicap parking spot is the mirage of the parking desert. You know the feeling. You see it in the distance, there it is. You can't believe your eyes, "It's too good to be true. A big, wide spot, and it's right by the entrance. Somehow everybody missed it." And then when you pull up, wait—it wasn't even there. There's nothing. It's like you were hallucinating. "I, I thought there was a spot there. I, I don't know what happened. . . . I—"

What is the handicap parking situation at the Special Olympics? They must have to just stack like a hundred cars into those two spots. How else can they do it?

Many states in the country now have traffic school to get a ticket taken off your license. I went to traffic school, I didn't mind it. I felt bad for the traffic school instructor. This guy goes to traffic school every day no matter how he drives. What is his incentive not to speed? He's going to traffic school anyway. Why not get a race car, do two hundred miles an hour down the street? Cop stops you, "Where are you going?"

"Traffic School."

"All right, go ahead. And you better hurry, you really need it."

Maybe the punishment should be instead of traffic school or traffic court, just traffic. They sentence you to one hundred hours of traffic. They assign like five people to drive all around you at five miles an hour wherever you go. You're on your way to Vegas, there isn't a car in sight, "Come on, move it!"

I was in front of an ambulance the other day, and I noticed that the word *ambulance* was spelled in reverse print on the hood of the ambulance. And I thought, "Well, isn't that clever." I look in the rearview mirror, I can read the word *ambulance* behind me. Of course while you're reading, you don't see where you're going, you crash, and you need an ambulance. I think maybe they're just trying to drum up some business on the way back from lunch.

You know what I never get with the limo? The tinted windows. Is that so people don't see you? Yeah, what better way not to have people notice you than taking a thirty foot Cadillac with a TV antenna and a uniformed driver. How discreet. Nobody cares who's in the limo anyway. You see a limo go by, you know it's either some rich jerk, or fifty prom kids with a dollar seventy-five each. A lot of people like to use that glass divider between the front, they like to put that up. Then you have to talk to the driver on the phone through the glass, so now what you have is a traveling prison visiting room. That feels good.

Being in the back of a limo, I'm sorry, it's just not that cool. Most of the time, I've felt like I'm in some depressing single guy's apartment from 1975. All that maroon velour furniture, couple of half-filled bottles of unknown liquor, three cassette tapes, all those mysterious stains . . . You're thinking, "There must've been ten thousand asses already on this seat."

The subway change-booth guy. I feel for this person. He's in a shark cage down there. It's this little safety chamber just floating in the subway. They give him like twenty-eight bucks in change, they seal him up inside this thing with bullet-proof glass, closed in on all sides, it's like some kind of Houdini torture tank of doom. How do you breathe in there? It looks like if you put your hand over the change slot, you could suffocate him in thirty seconds.

So I take the subway down to Coney Island to go on the Cyclone. Here I am, I'm sitting on the "D" train for an hour and fifteen minutes, so I can go on a scary ride. How dumb is that? You know that first sharp drop on the Cyclone? I fell asleep. It was the least exciting part of my day.

LOOK, UP IN THE AIR!

I'm not afraid of flying, although many people do have a fear of flying and I have no argument with that.

I think fear of flying is quite rational because, human beings cannot fly. Humans should have fear of flying the same way fish should have fear of driving. Put a fish behind the wheel and they probably go, "This isn't right. I shouldn't be doing this. I don't belong here."

Do you think that the people at the airport that run the stores have any idea what the prices are every place else in the world? Or do you think they just feel they have their own little country out there and they can charge anything they want?

"Little hungry? You want a tuna sandwich? It's 28 dollars. If you don't like it, go back to your own country." I think the whole airport/airline complex is a huge scam just to sell the tuna sandwiches. I think that tuna profit is what's supporting the entire air-travel industry. The planes could fly empty, they'd still make money. The terminals, the airplanes, the parking, the giftshops, it's all just to distract you so you don't notice the beating you're taking on the tuna.

I believe the closest thing that we have to royalty in America are the people that get to ride in those little carts through the airport.

Don't you hate these things? They come out of nowhere. "Beep, beep. Cart people, look out, cart people!" We all scurry out of the way like worthless peasants. "Ooh, it's cart people. I hope we didn't slow you down. Wave to the cart people, Timmy. They're the best people in the world." If you're too fat, slow, and disoriented to get to your gate in time, you're not ready for air travel.

The other people I hate are the people that get onto the moving walkway and then just stand there. Like it's a ride. "Excuse me, there's no animated pirates or bears along the way here. Do your legs work at all?"

I was on a plane the other day, and I was wondering, "Are there keys to the plane? Do they need keys to start the plane?"

Maybe that's what those delays on the ground are sometimes, when you're just sitting there at the gate. Maybe the pilot sits up there in the cockpit going, "Oh I don't believe this. . . . dammit . . . I did it again." They tell you it's something mechanical, because they don't want to come on the P.A. system, "Ladies and gentlemen, we're going to be delayed here on the ground for a little while. I uh . . . Oh, God, this is so embarrassing. . . . I, I left the keys to the plane in my apartment. They're in this big blue ashtray by the front door. I'm really sorry. I'll run back and get them."

You see the technicians all running around underneath the plane. You think they're servicing it, but they're actually looking for one of those magnet Hide-A-Keys under the wing.

I'm on the plane, we left late, and the pilot says, "We're going to be making up some time in the air." I thought, "Isn't that interesting. They just make up time." That's why you have to reset your watch when you land.

Of course, when they say they're making up time, obviously they're increasing the speed of the aircraft. Now my question is, if you can go faster, why don't you just go as fast as you can all the time? "Come on, there're no cops up here! Nail it! Give it some gas! We're flying!"

You can measure distance by time.

"How far away is that place?"

"About 20 minutes." But it doesn't work the other way.

"When do you get off work?"

"Around 3 miles."

JERRY SEINFELD

I love those small airplane bathrooms. It's like your own little apartment on the plane. You go in, you close the door, the light comes right on. It's a little surprise party every time you go in.

And I love the sign in the airplane bathroom. "As a courtesy to the next passenger, please wipe off the counter with your towel." Well, let me earn my wings every day. Sorry, I forgot to bring my toilet-bowl brush with me. When did this Brotherhood of Passengers get started? "Did they lose your luggage? Here take mine. We're all passengers together. By the way, was that bathroom clean enough for you? I couldn't find the Comet or I would've had that crapper gleaming."

Everything on planes is very tiny.

There's always tiny food, tiny liquor bottles, tiny pillows, tiny bathroom, tiny sink, tiny soap. Everyone's in a cramped seat, working on a tiny computer. There's always "a small problem, there'll be a slight delay, we'll be a bit late, if you can be a little patient. We're just trying to get one of those little trucks to pull us up a little closer to the jetway so you can walk down the narrow hallway. There'll be a man there in a tight little jacket and he'll tell you that you have very little time to make your connecting flight. So move it!"

So I was on this plane where it was this flight attendant's first day on the job, but they didn't have a uniform for her yet. And that really makes a big difference. I mean, now it's just some regular person coming over to you going, "Would you mind bringing your seatback all the way up?"

I turned around, "Who the hell are you?"

And then she goes, "Well, I'm the flight attendant."

"Oh yeah? Then I'm the pilot. Why don't you sit down, I'm about to bring her in."

I don't know why people always have the same reaction when they hear about a plane crash.

"Plane crash? What airline?"

"Where was it going?"

As if it makes a difference, like you're going to go, "Oh, *that* flight. Oh, okay, that I can understand." Like there's some planes that are *expected* to crash.

You go up to the ticket agent. "Excuse me, this flight generally goes down quite a bit, doesn't it?"

JERRY SEINFELD

"Actually it does, yes. We do have another flight, but it explodes on take-off. It is, however, a snack flight."

Flying doesn't make me nervous. Driving to the airport can make me nervous. Because if you miss that plane, there's no alternative. On the ground you have options. You have buses, you have taxis, you have trains.

But when you're taking a flight, if you miss it, that's it. No airline goes, "Well, you missed the flight. We do have a cannon leaving in about ten minutes. Would you be interested in that? It's not a direct cannon, you have to change cannons after you land." "So all right, let's aim it here, where are you going, Chicago? Oh Dallas, all right, wait a second then, let me move it a little. Dallas, that's about Dallas . . . Texas, anyway. You should hit Texas. Are you ready? Now, make sure you get out of the net immediately because we shoot the luggage in right after you."

The worst way of flying, I think, is standby. You ever fly standby? It never works. That's why they call it standby. You end up standing there going, "Bye."

Oh and hey, one last thing.

Attention all flight attendants: Stop waking us up on the planes to eat your crummy food. If we're sleeping, let us sleep. Would you want to be awakened in your bed to eat a runny omelet? No. Nobody wants to be woken up for anything. You eat when you get up. What is the God damn emergency? You think you have the only food in the world? If I miss the barf buffet altogether, so what? *Food is available elsewhere.* We don't care about it. Who the hell trains you people? Have they *ever* flown?

Remember: Of the two things you might do on a plane, sleeping is extremely difficult. Eating is very, very easy. If we've accomplished the hard one, don't come shaking us to do the moron one, namely, eating your little crap cakes.

We want to get where we're going and hopefully not be totally exhausted. That's what's important to us. Your hideous little trays of fly-slop are a necessary evil—that's all. Get these priorities straight immediately. Are we clear?

Thank you.

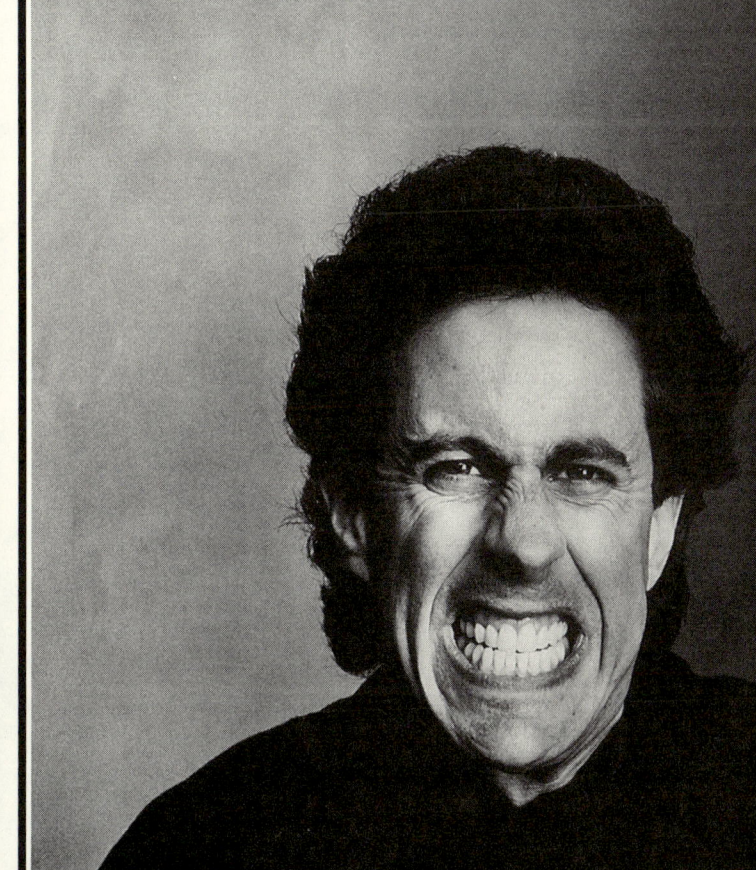

JOB SECURITY

There are so many jobs, occupations, and ways to make a living. And every person goes into a job thinking they're getting away with something, that it's not really hard to do. Or the hours. Or they think the money's pretty good.

Basically the only incentive a person needs to accept a job is to be shown another job where the work is the same but the pay is a little less.

Then their job automatically becomes what is referred to as "not a bad job." That's really all we want—

a "not a bad job"—and we're happy.

Some people will say they've got a "great job." These people are being significantly overpaid. The IRS needs to go after these people that think they have a great job.

There's the answer to your deficit.

And these people are annoying anyway.

"Oh yeah? You've got a great job? Well guess what, starting Monday you're only getting paid every other week.

How great is it now?"

Nobody likes the great job people. They're almost as reviled as the great apartment people.

OFFICE SPACE

I've never really had an actual job. I've worked. But I don't know much about the job thing.

To me, the most annoying thing about the couple of times that I worked in an office is that when you show up in the morning you say "hi" to everyone and then for some reason, you have to continue to greet these people all day every time you see them. You walk in at the start of the day, "Morning, Bill, morning, Bob. How are you doing?" "Fine."

Ten minutes later you see them in the hall, again you say, "How you doing?" Now, I already know how he's doing, I just saw him, he told me how he's doing. But you've got to keep saying something each time you pass. So you keep coming up with different little greetings. You start coming up with nicknames for them. . . . "Jimbo." You do the little smile with the head raise. The almost imperceptible beneath-the-breath "Hey" with a half-smile. If it's a narrow passageway, thank God now you can say, "Excuse me." But it has to have a very friendly singsong quality. You kind of go up a note on the "me." If you feel more familiar, "Tight squeeze" is popular. When walking by a group of 3 or more men, "Gentlemen" is often used to confer an air of sophistication that is always misplaced.

Day-of-the-week references are always good, especially Monday or Friday because of the obligatory emotions that are assumed to go with them. Any mention of weekend seems to comfort people. "Good weekend?" "Have a good weekend?" People like anything with weekend in it. Thursday's good for "One more day," which usually prompts the easy "You said it" rejoinder. Wednesday, "Humpday."

"That it is."

We should all agree that we're just going to say, "Acknowledge" as we pass people in the halls. You know, just walk by, "Acknowledge, acknowledge." We'll become Vulcans for four seconds and not have to wrack our brains every time we just want to go to the bathroom.

I was watching this movie the other night. It was a World War Two movie and there were Nazis in the movie. And I notice that the Nazis in those movies always had two separate "Heil's." They had the regular "Heil" that they would do, and then, when they were around the offices, they had this casual "Heil," where they would just kind of show their palm. Remember that? They come in the office, "Yeah, Heil, how are you? Is the kid back with the coffee yet? Are you finished with the copier? Yeah, world domination, Aryan race, whose donuts are those? Yeah, Heil, nice to see you. Mind if I take the last jelly?"

Frankly, I don't believe people think of their office as a workplace anyway. I think they think of it as a stationery store with Danish. You want to get your pastry, your envelopes, your supplies, your toilet paper, six cups of coffee, and you go home.

I like almost any kind of work. I don't know what my problem is. But I've learned to kind of keep this fact quiet as it seems to make people uncomfortable. That's one great thing about show business—the word *work* has a completely different connotation. In show business, if you're working it's a good thing. If you're not working it's a bad thing. Just the reverse of normal jobs.

There's always a tremendous peer pressure around workplaces to assume that everybody hates working, hates their job, and every second they're at work is pure pain.

Why do people who work in offices have pictures of their family on their desk facing them? Do they forget that they're married? Do they say to themselves, "All right. Five o'clock. Time to hit the bars and pick up some hookers. Hold it a second, look at this picture. I got a wife and three kids. I completely forgot! I better get home."

LAWMEN

What are lawyers really? To me a lawyer is basically the person that knows the rules of the country. We're all throwing the dice, playing the game, moving our pieces around the board, but if there's a problem, the lawyer is the only person that has actually read the inside of the top of the box.

I think probably the most fun thing a lawyer can do is say, "Objection."

"Objection! Objection, Your Honor!"

Objection, of course, is the adult version of " 'fraid not!" To which the judge can say two things. He can say, "Overruled," which is the adult version of " 'Fraid so." Or he can say "Sustained," which is the adult version of "Duh."

I could enjoy a career in law enforcement. Don't you love catching someone trying to get away with something? I love it. But that's why I could never be a cop because I would be too happy. I would catch somebody speeding and go, "I got you, I got you, I got you. Eighty miles an hour, I got you. . . ." Really obnoxious.

People like to catch people. That's why in the Old West they had the posse because everybody wanted to be involved in apprehending the outlaw. Now, you probably couldn't have the posse today because people don't have time for it and they have phone machines so they could screen the calls.

"Yeah, Bill, this is Jim. We're trying to get a posse together. Bill? Are you there? . . . Bill, c'mon, pick it up. . . . I know you're there. . . . Come on, one posse. . . . Please Bill, pick up the phone, we're trying to form a posse."

Aren't you a little surprised that cops still have to read that whole "You have the right to remain silent" speech to every criminal they arrest? I mean is there anybody who doesn't know that by now? Can't they just go, "Freeze, you're under arrest. You ever seen *Baretta*?"

"Yeah."

"Good, get in the car."

There are many different jobs for cops these days. It seems to me that Chalk Outline Guy is one of the better jobs that you can get. It's not too dangerous, the criminals are long gone—that seems like a good one.

I don't know who these guys are. I guess they're people who wanted to be sketch artists but they couldn't draw too well. "Uh, listen Johnson, forget the sketches, do you think if we left the dead body right there on the sidewalk, you could manage to trace around it? Could you do that?"

I don't even know how that helps them solve the crime. They look at the thing on the ground, "Oh, his arm was like that when he hit the pavement, that means the killer must have been . . . Jim."

FIRST AID

What do you think first aid was like hundreds of years ago? I mean, they had no medicine, no drugs, no technology, no equipment. Basically, they were there first. That was it. That was the whole first aid. They sat with you, that's all they could do.

"Can you help me?"

"No, no, we can't help you. But we were the first ones here, I don't know if you know that. Did you see our truck? 'First Aid,' that's our motto. We show up before anybody."

People love to recommend their doctor to you. I don't know what they get out of it, but they really push them on you.

"Is he good?"

"He's the best. This guy's the best." There can't be this many "bests." Someone's graduating at the bottom of these classes. Where are these doctors? Is someone somewhere saying to their friend, "You should see my doctor, he's the worst. He's the absolute worst there is. Whatever you've got, it'll be worse after you see him. The man's an absolute butcher."

And whenever a friend refers a doctor they say, "Make sure that you tell him that you know me." Why? What's the difference? He's a doctor.

"Oh, you know Bob? Oh, okay, I'll give you the *real* medicine. Everybody else I'm giving Tic Tacs."

I hate the waiting room because it's called the waiting room so there's no chance of not waiting. It's built, designed, and intended for waiting. Why would they take you right away when they've got this room all set up? And you sit there with your little magazine. You pretend you're reading it but you're really looking at the other people. "I wonder what he's got." Then they finally call you, and you think you're going to see the doctor, but you're not. You're going into the next smaller waiting room. Now you don't even have your magazine. You've got no pants on. You're looking at colon-cancer brochures, peeking out the blinds.

But medically speaking, it's always good to be in a small room. You don't want to be in a large room. Have you ever seen these operating theaters that they have with stadium seating? You don't want them doing anything to you that makes other doctors go, "Well, I have to see this. Are you kidding? Are they really going to do that? Are there seats? Can we get in?"

I wonder if they ever have scalp tickets to an operation? "I got two for the Winslow tumor, who needs two?"

(By the way, don't think I didn't see the scalp tickets-scalpel joke opportunity. I just passed. If you'd like to make one, be my guest.)

Doctor forms are getting more involved, aren't they? It used to be "measles, mumps, allergic to penicillin." Now it's like, "What was the home address of your former employer? What was the name of the black guy on *Ironsides*?" What do they need to know all this stuff for?

And it's so hard to write with those little golf pencils that they give you. I guess they're not making enough money ripping us off, they've got to steal the pencils from the golf course too. That's why they have to go every Wednesday, to get more pencils.

I'm always afraid to get something in that little box they have labeled, "For office use only." What goes in there? I think they use it as a coaster for their drinks while they're reading it over. "Hey Ed, check it out, this guy's got some weird stuff happening. . . . Oh, you can put your drink down there, on that box."

And why does the pharmacist have to be two and a half feet up above everybody else? Who the hell is he? He's a stockboy with pills as far as I can tell. Why can't he be down there on the floor with you and me? Brain surgeons, airline pilots, nuclear physicists, we're all on the same level. But not him. He's gotta be two and a half feet up. "Look out, everybody, I'm working with pills up here. Spread out, gimme some room. I'm taking them from this big bottle and I'm putting them in this little bottle."

The only hard part of his whole job that I can see is typing everything onto that little, tiny label. He has to get a lot of words on there plus keep that small paper in the roller of the typewriter. That impresses me. But putting pills in a bottle with a white jacket on, I don't know why you need a diploma for that.

Then there's the psychiatrist. Why is it that with the psychiatrist every hour is only fifty minutes? What do they do with that ten minutes that they have left? Do they just sit there going, "Boy that guy was crazy. I couldn't believe the things he was saying. What a nut. Who's coming in next? Oh no, another head case."

And who's keeping track of the psychics? Psychics should be licensed. It wouldn't be hard. We could just give them the regular DMV test, only with silver dollars and the pizza dough over the eyes. I mean, if you can do the parallel park like that, you're a psychic.

We can test these people, there's no question about it. Like Kreskin, instead of just hiding the check, why don't we try stopping his check? Let's see how he handles that.

ENTERTAINERS

The hardest part of being a clown, it seems to me, would be that you are constantly referred to as a clown. "Who is that clown?" "I'm not working with that clown." "Did you hire that clown?" "The guy's a clown."

How do you even know that you want to be a clown? I guess you just get to a point where your pants look so bad it's actually easier to become a clown than have the proper alterations done.

JERRY SEINFELD

Because if you think about it, a clown, if there isn't a circus around them, is really just a very annoying person. I mean, you're in the back seat of this guy's Volkswagen. "What, you're picking more people up? Oh man!"

Talk-show hosts never seem to have any idea how much time is left in the show, you know? They're always looking off camera, "Do we have time? Are we out of time? How we doing on time?"

You never see Magnum P.I. go, "Should I strangle this guy or are we gonna take a break here? Can you stay for another beating? I'll tell you what, I'll bop him in the head, we'll do a commercial, we'll come back, I'll drive in the car real fast. Stay with us."

I don't think anything competes with a magic act for humiliating entertainment value.

What is the point of the magician? He comes on, he fools you, you feel stupid, show's over. You never know what's actually happened. It's never explained. And that's kind of the attitude the magician seems to have as he's performing.

It's like, "Here's a quarter. Now it's gone. You're a

jerk." Sometimes they ask you to blow on it. There's something mature adults like to do, blow on a deck of cards. I also love that little pretend look of surprise they do when the trick works. Like, "Oh, I didn't know that was going to happen myself. I even amaze me."

Las Vegas is still the ultimate entertainment town to me. Somebody explains everything to you there.

You come in the hotel, the bellhop takes you upstairs, explains to you how to use the TV.

You turn on the TV, there's a guy on there explains to you how to go downstairs and play the games.

You play the games, you go out on the sidewalk and there's a girl out there to explain to you how to go upstairs and use the room again.

And you keep going until you run out of girls or games or money, and then you go home.

Unemployment, that's a tough thing.

Even if you get a job, after you've been unemployed, they take unemployment out of your check every week and show it to you in that little box. How good can it be

JERRY SEINFELD

for your confidence that every paycheck has the word "unemployment" on it? You can't get it out of your mind. You just got the job, they're already getting ready for you to be laid off.

I have a friend who's unemployed—he's collecting unemployment insurance. This guy has never worked so hard in his life as he has to keep this thing going. He's down there every week, waiting on the lines and getting interviewed and making up all these lies about looking for jobs.

If they had any idea of the effort and energy that he is expending to avoid work, I'm sure they'd give him a raise.

I've never seen someone do such a tremendous job, not working.

THE THING IS THE THING

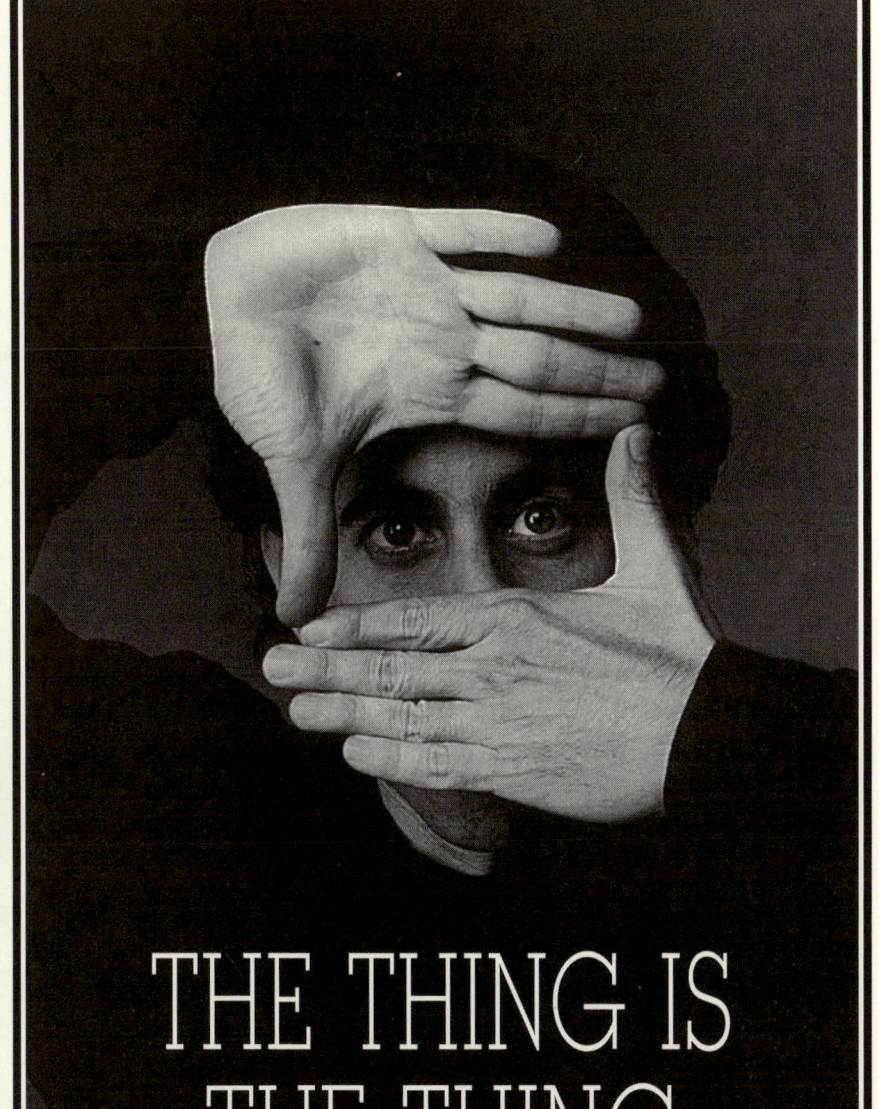

Like it or not our things represent us. Most of the time, people's things even look like them. Everyone is in the perfect clothes for them no matter what they are. To me everything you have is really a layer of clothing. Your body is your innermost and truest outfit. Your house is another layer of wardrobe. Then your neighborhood, your city, your state. It's all one giant outfit. We're wearing everything. That's why in certain towns, no matter what you've got on, you're a bad dresser. Just for being there. Some places you're better off just moving instead of changing.

MY MONEY'S NOT WORKING

I have not done well as an investor.

In fact, I have lost money on virtually every investment I've ever made. A lot of times I've lost everything I put in.

People always tell me, "You should have your money working for you." Well, from now on, I've decided I'll do the work, I'm going to let my money relax. Because who knows what your money has been through before it got to you? Maybe it's been working. Maybe it's tired. Maybe that's why it left where it was. Maybe if I'm nice to it, it'll stay with me.

I hate when they call up to check if your credit card is good.

I always feel like they're talking about me. "You won't believe what he's buying now. It's some kind of yellow thing. I don't even know what it is, we've never sold one before. Get down here right away, I'll try and stall him."

JERRY SEINFELD

The main difference between the man's wallet and the woman's wallet is the photo section. Women carry with them a photograph of every person they've ever met every day in their whole life since the beginning of time. And every picture's out of date. "Here's my cousin, 3 years old, she's in the Marines now. This is my dog, he died during the Carter administration." They get stopped by a cop, no license, no registration. "Here's my fifty-six people who know me." Cop goes, "All right, ma'am, just wanted to make sure you had some friends. Move it along . . . Routine pal check."

Which is really crushing our lives more? Paying the taxes or doing the taxes? I think it's close. To me, the sad thing about doing your taxes is when you realize all you have to show for a whole year of activity is a shoe box full of receipts. Then I empty it out and start January 1 filling it up again. This is what I'm doing with my life. I'm filling up shoe boxes with little pieces of paper and showing it to the government.

I wish instead of doing my taxes I could just take my shoe box to Washington, D.C., right to the I.R.S. And just go, "Here, look. It's the same box as last year. Do we have to go through all this again?"

But what do I get for all the money I spend on taxes? I don't have any kids, I don't use the school system. I don't use the police, the prisons. I've never called the military. Basically, I use the post office and the white lines on the road. A third of my working life for postcards and driving straight.

I was audited last year. I have been through an audit.

Even though I.R.S. kind of sounds like Toys 'R' Us, they're not fun people. There's things they could do to liven up the audit. I think they should take all your receipts and put them in one of those big, lucite sweepstakes drums, and just crank it around—you know, give you a feeling like you might win something. Then they can pull 'em out one by one and go, "Oh, I'm sorry. That's another illegal deduction. But we do have some lovely parting gifts for you. . . . Jail."

THE CRIMINAL LIFE

I have not been to jail. But I think about jail a lot. I don't know why. I think about how I would fix up my cell. How many push-ups I would do.

JERRY SEINFELD

Because I live alone anyway, it's kind of the same. I'm in solitary.

How can you not think about jail? Every night on TV we watch people going there. Whenever they're hauling in some criminal terrorist, psycho, mass-murderer guy, you notice he's always covering up his face with the newspaper, a jacket, a hat.

What is this man's reputation that he has to worry about this kind of exposure damaging his good name? Is he up for a big job promotion down at the office or something? Afraid the boss is going to catch this on TV and go, "Isn't that Johnson from sales? He was up in that clock tower picking people off one-by-one. I don't know if that's the kind of man we want heading up that new branch office. He should be in bill collection."

I got ripped off for about the eighteenth time recently. And one of your friends will always say, "Call the police. You really should call the police."

So you think to yourself, "Yeah, I'm calling the police." Because you watch TV. "Stakeouts, manhunts. We'll see some real action." So the police come over to your house, they fill out the report, they give you . . .

your copy. Now, unless they give the crook his copy, I don't really think we're going to crack this case, do you?

It's not like Batman where there's three crooks in the city, and everybody pretty much knows who they are. Very few crooks even go to the trouble to come up with a theme for their careers anymore. It makes them a lot tougher to spot. "They stole a CD player out of your car? It could be the Penguin. I think we'll be able to round him up. He's dressed like a penguin."

To me, now and forever, Superman is the guy. If there's only one guy, this is the guy. There's no other guys, there's no better guys, there's nobody competing with this guy, I don't care if he's dead, alive, quadrupled, under a red sun, yellow sun, he's Superman and that's it, case closed.

But of all the Supermans, comic books, movies, cartoons, George Reeves will always be my favorite. Because the real thing about being Superman, the thing that makes it so interesting is it's a thing you're saddled with. On his planet he was normal. But here, he's Superman. And it was that way for George Reeves. Being Superman was a thing he just ended up with.

Did he want to be Superman? Maybe, maybe not. But

JERRY SEINFELD

he was Superman. He looked like a guy who got stuck being Superman. The padded outfits, the bad scripts, the phony-looking sets. He dealt with it all. He had to, he was Superman. And that's what you do when you're Superman. You come in every week, and you try to be Super. Someone had to try to make the stupid show work.

Maybe I love Superman because I love remembering when I could buy the whole thing. And nothing tested your faith like the TV show.

Here's my short list of questions: Where were the other reporters on the *Daily Planet*? Where were the other police besides Inspector Henderson? Why were the crooks always, and only, in groups of two, a dumb one and a smart one? Often with names like "Lefty" and "The Boss." Who was "The Boss" the boss of? Lefty? How good a disguise is a pair of glasses? And with no lenses in the frames of the glasses? Why did Superman have no feet in the opening sequence? What was that planet in the background that looked like a "C"? Who was Clark always winking at in the end? Me? Why? I'm not there, I'm watching TV. Why destroy the tissue-thin believability even more after I just invested 30 minutes? And most of all, why didn't Superman ever just tell Lois and Jimmy, "Look, you're not helping. You're only making my job harder. Would you both please just let me deal with crooks? Believe me, I can handle it."

But when you want to enjoy something, you must never let logic get too much in the way. Like the villains in all the James Bond movies. Whenever Bond breaks into the complex: "Ah, Mr. Bond, welcome, come in. Let me show you my entire evil plan and then put you in a death machine that doesn't work."

The other odd thing about the Bond movies is they have the most evil guy in the world vs. the most good guy in the world and you leave liking both of them equally.

Do the security guards in the art museums really ever stop anybody from taking the paintings? I mean are they going up to the thieves, "Hey, hey, hey, where do you think you're going with that? Hey, come over here, give me that Cézanne." I mean look at the job that this man is hired to do. He's getting five dollars an hour to protect millions of dollars of priceless art and with what? He's got a light mocha brown uniform and a *USA Today*. This is all he's got. I mean crooks must look at this guy and go,

JERRY SEINFELD

"Alright all we gotta do is get past the folding chair and the thermos of coffee and we can get a Rembrandt."

The fact of life is that people will try and take your possessions. People are going to steal from you. Everybody has their own little personal security things. Things that they think will foil the crooks. You go to the beach, go into the water, put your wallet in the sneaker . . . Who's going to know? What criminal mind could penetrate this fortress of security? I tied a bow. They can't get through that. I put it down by the toe. They never look there. They check the heels, they move on.

Or, you ever move a TV set in the back of your car? Then you've got to leave the car in the street for a few minutes, you put a sweater over the TV. "It's a couple of sweaters, that's all. One of them happens to be square with an antenna coming out of it. It's an RCA sweater."

MEDIA MEZZO

To me the worst thing about television is that everybody you see on television is doing something better than what you're doing. You never see anybody on TV just sliding off the front of the sofa with potato chip crumbs all over their shirt.

Some people are having a little too much fun on television. The soda commercial people—where do they get this enthusiasm? Have you seen them? "We have soda, we have soda, we have soda!" Jumping, laughing, flying through the air. It's a can of soda.

Have you ever been sitting there watching TV and you're drinking the exact same product that they're advertising right there on TV? And they're spiking volleyballs, jet skiing, girls in bikinis. And you're sitting there, "Maybe I'm putting too much ice in mine. I'm not getting *that* effect."

Don't you hate "To Be Continued"s on TV? It's horrible when you sense the "To Be Continued" coming. You know you're watching the show, you're into the story, then there's like five minutes left and suddenly you realize, "Hey, they can't make it. Timmy's still stuck in the cave. There's no way they can wrap this up in five minutes." I mean the whole reason you watch a TV show is because it ends. If I wanted a long, boring story with no point to it, I've got my life. A comedian can't do that. I can't go, "A

JERRY SEINFELD

man walks into a bar with a pig under his arm . . . Can you come back next week?"

TV has so much power. I know it does. Because I bought the Ginsu knife. I did. The Ginsu 2000, actually. I can't believe I did it.

I can't believe I wrote the number down.

I can't believe I called it.

I can't believe I gave them my credit card number.

It was late at night, I was watching the commercial and it started making sense to me. The guy cuts through the can, cuts through the shoe. I'm thinking, "That looks pretty good."

I don't think I can cut through a shoe with any of my knives. What if I get a knot in the laces and I can't get out of my shoe?

How am I going to get out?

I'll have to cut my way out.

I need that knife.

So I called up and incredible as it may seem, I actually spoke these words. I said, "I would like to order the Ginsu knife." Yes, I said it. And the lady on the phone just went, "Really?"

Even the Ginsu people can't believe anybody would actually want this thing.

So now I have it, my shoes are all cut in half and I don't watch TV late at night anymore.

I will never understand why they cook on TV.

I can't smell it.

Can't eat it.

Can't taste it.

The end of the show they hold it up to the camera, "Well, here it is. You can't have any. Thanks for watching. Goodbye."

I hate these public service TV spots where they try to get you to sign your organ donor card on your license.

"Little Jimmy here needs an organ transplant. He can't do anything but wait, and hope for you to do something really stupid. So sign that card and you know, maybe start thinking about that high-powered motorcycle for yourself. There's nothing like feeling that wind whipping through your hair, no helmet, flying down the road."

JERRY SEINFELD

There are many things you can point to as proof that the human is not smart. But my personal favorite would have to be that we needed to invent the helmet. What was happening, apparently, was that we were involved in a lot of activities that were cracking our heads. We chose *not* to avoid doing these activities but, instead, to come up with some sort of device to help us continue enjoying our head-cracking lifestyles. The helmet. And even that didn't work because not enough people were wearing them so we had to come up with the helmet law. Which is even stupider, the idea behind the helmet law being to preserve a brain whose judgment is so poor, it does not even try to stop the cracking of the head it's in.

Men seem to flip around the television more than women. Men get that remote control in their hands, they don't even know what the hell they're not watching. You know we just keep going, "Rerun, that's stupid, he's stupid, she's stupid, go, go, go."

"What are you watching?"

"I don't care, I gotta keep going."

"Who was that?"

"I don't know what it was, doesn't matter, it's not your fault, I gotta keep going."

"I think that's a documentary on your father."

"Don't care, what else is on?"

Women don't do this. Women will stop and go, "Well let me see what the show is, before I change the channel. Maybe we can nurture it, work with it, help it grow into something." Men don't do that. Because women nest and men hunt. That's why we watch TV differently.

Before there was flipping around, before there was television, kings and emperors and pharaohs had storytellers. That was their entertainment. I wonder if they ever would get like thirty storytellers together so they could flip around. Just go, "All right, start telling me a story, what's happening? . . . I don't want to hear anymore. Shut up. Go to the next guy. What are you talking about? . . . Is there a girl in that story . . . no? Shut up. Go to the next guy. What do you got? . . . I don't want to hear that either. Shut up . . . No go ahead, what are you talking about, I don't wanna hear that. . . . No, forget it all of you, get out of here. I'm going to bed."

Magazines are another medium I love because, like TV, 95% of it is simply based on "How the hell are we going to fill all this blank space?"

You can always tell it's a slow news week when you

see articles like, "Did Comets Kill the Dinosaurs?" Here's a hot topic—who's got time for this? "Hey, what happened to the dinosaurs? Weren't they just here?"

Maybe comets killed the dinosaurs, maybe they tripped and fell. What's the difference? We'll never know.

We couldn't solve the Kennedy Assassination, we had films of that. Good luck with the Stegosaurus.

"Round up all these reptiles for questioning, Bill. I want to talk with that little salamander over there. I think he knows something. Don't stick your tongue out at me, young man. I'll nail your slimy little butt to the wall."

Sunday paper is the worst. Weekend. You want to relax. "Oh, by the way, here's a thousand pages of information you had no idea about." How can they tell you everything they know every single day of the week and then have this much left over on Sunday when nothing's going on?

I have to tell you that I did get some very exciting news recently, and I don't know if I should really tell you exactly what it is because it's really not a definite thing yet. . . . All right, well, I will tell you what I do know so far.

According to the information that I have, in the envelope that I received, it seems . . . that I may have already won some very valuable prizes. Thank you, thank you very much. Now remember, they're not saying anything definitely yet. To be honest with you, I didn't even know I was in this thing.

But according to the readout, it looks like I am among the top people that they are considering. It's certainly very exciting and I will keep you apprised as soon as I hear anything else. I have to send some stuff in. I don't know exactly how it works, but it looks pretty good so far.

That's what annoys me about sweepstakes companies, they always tease you with that, "You may have already won," and we all buy into it. "Hey, maybe I have, maybe it's all over, maybe I'm the big winner and I don't even know."

I'd like once for a sweepstakes company to have some guts, come out with the truth, just be honest with people one time. Send out envelopes, "You have definitely lost." You turn it over, giant printing, "Not even close!" You open it up, there's this whole letter of explanation, "Even we cannot believe how badly you've done on this contest. Where the hell was your head when you filled out these forms? You have no luck, you'll never win anything, get out of our face, stop bothering us, you're a big loser, we hate you, good-bye."

Fear of success is one of the new fears I've heard about lately. And I think it's definitely a sign that we're running out of fears. A person suffering from fear of success is scraping the bottom of the fear barrel.

Are we going to need AA-type meetings for these people? They get up to the microphone and go, "Hi, my name is Bill and I can't stand the thought of having a stereo and a cream colored couch."

According to most studies, people's number one fear is public speaking. Number two is death. Death is number two. Does that seem right? That means to the average person, if you have to go to a funeral, you're better off in the casket than doing the eulogy.

The thing I don't understand about the suicide person is the people who try to commit suicide, for some reason they don't die, and that's it. They stop trying. Why don't they just keep trying? What's changed? Is their life any better now? No. In fact, it's worse, because now they've found out here's one more thing you stink at. And that's why these people don't succeed at life to begin with. They give up too easy.

I say, pills don't work? Try a rope. Car won't start in the garage? Get a tune-up. There's nothing more rewarding than reaching a goal you've set for yourself.

OUT AND BACK

You can divide your whole life into two basic categories.

You're either staying in or going out.

Everything else is irrelevant detail.

The urge to go out and then return is very strong. Just look at what happens to people when they don't want to stay home and they have to. They become despondent. Or if someone's locked out of their house and can't get in when they want? They go nuts.

We must go out. We must go back.

When you're out, everything's a little out of control and exciting. Something could happen. You might see something. You might find out something. You might even be a part of something. We've got to go out there.

When you're back in your house you're like the conductor of an orchestra. You know where everything is and how to work it. You move confidently from one part of your house to another. You know exactly where you're going and what will happen when you get there.

You're the maestro of a symphony with nothing on but socks and underwear.

And it's because we know it so well that we've got to get out.

DINING OUT

Went out to dinner the other night, check came at the end of the meal as it always does. Never liked the check at the end of the meal system. Because money's a very different thing before and after you eat.

Before you eat, money has very little value. When you're hungry, you sit down in a restaurant, you're like the ruler of an empire. You don't care about cost. You want maximum food in minimum time.

"More drinks, appetizers, quickly, quickly. Fried things in the shape of a stick or a ball. It will be the greatest meal of our lives."

Then, after the meal, once you're full, you can't remember ever being hungry ever in your life. You see people walking in the restaurant, you can't believe it. "Why are these people coming in here now? I'm so full. How could they eat?" You've got the pants undone, napkins destroyed, cigarette butt in the mashed potatoes. You never want to see food again as long as you live. That's when the check comes. This is why people are always mystified by the check.

"What is this? How could this be?" They start passing it around the table.

"Does this look right to you? We're not hungry now, why are we buying all this food?"

Sometimes you go to a nice restaurant, they put the check in the little book. What is this, the story of the bill? "Once upon a time somebody ordered a salad." There's a little gold tassel hanging down. Am I graduating from the restaurant? Should I put this on the rearview mirror of my Camaro?

Everybody wants to know everybody's diet, "You look O.K., what do you eat?" Here's mine:

Basically, I eat pretty good. But if I'm hungry and there's something in front of me, I eat that. When I get back to a hotel late at night after doing a show, if there's a room-service tray in the hallway and there's a roll on it that doesn't look too bad . . . I might eat it. I figure what are the odds somebody in a hotel room would go, "Hey, before we put the tray out, let's poison a roll and then leave it in the hall in case there's a comic coming back to his room at two o'clock in the morning—we can kill him."

Hunger will make people do amazing things. I mean, the proof of that is cannibalism. What do they say? You know, they're eating . . . "This is good. Who is this? I like this person." I would think the hardest thing about being a cannibal is trying to get some really solid straight through the night sleep. You'd think with any little noise they'd go "What is it? . . . Who's that? . . . Who's there? . . . Is somebody there? . . . What do you want? . . . You look hungry. Are you hungry? . . . Get out of here."

The Constitution forbids cruel and unusual punishment. Personally, I'd be more concerned about the unusual. And I think our treatment of the lobster definitely falls into that category.

It's not enough that we catch them, kill them, and eat them. We want to see them in the tank as we walk into the restaurant, sweating it out. They actually look nervous.

I saw one once that looked like he was attempting to clean the inside of the tank. "I just work here." The other lobsters were laughing at him. "Go ahead and laugh, I've been here nine years. See those two little ones? Those are my boys. Newburg and Bisque."

Whenever you ask for the doggie bag at a restaurant, there's a certain sense of failure there, isn't there? People always whisper it to the waiter, "Uh, excuse me. Can I get the doggie bag? I, uh, I—I couldn't make it." It's embarrassing, because the doggie bag means either you're out at a restaurant when you're not hungry, or you've chosen the stupidest possible way there is to get dog food.

How about the doggie bag on a date? There's a good move. Let me tell you, if you're a guy and you ask for the doggie bag on a date, you might as well just have them wrap up your genitals too. You're not going to be needing them for a while, either.

WATCHING OUT

I went to an opera recently.

I've never really understood the importance of the orchestra conductor. I mean between you and me, what the hell is this guy doing? Do you really need somebody waving a stick in your face to play the violin? Does that really help you out? I could see how we need him at the beginning, okay? Tap, tap, tap, "ready and everyone *start.*" But once it's all going, what's he doing then? I don't see the cellist looking around going, "I'm confused, I don't know what to do. I'm lost." And the conductor waves the stick at him, "Do this, like this, like this," and he's, "Oh, okay, thank you, thank you very much. Now I've got it."

A lot of people had those little opera glasses. Do you really need the binos? How big do these people have to get before you can spot them? I mean these opera kids, they're going two-fifty, two-eighty, three twenty-five. They're wearing big, white, woolly vests. The women have the breast plates, the bullet hats, the horns coming out. If you can't pick these people out, forget opera. Think about optometry. Maybe that's more your thing.

At the complete opposite end of the physique spectrum, I once went to a runway-model fashion show. In fact they played some opera in the show. That worked. "Let's listen to those people and look at these people. Now you've got something." Although I must say I feel the whole concept of models and modeling is counterproductive to the fashion industry. Because when these women are around, who's looking at the clothes? I didn't notice any of the clothes. We're all applauding, "Oh wonderful, lovely." What are we applauding? We're applauding, "There's a lot of great looking women here, and we're here too." That's what we're applauding. "We're all in the same room together. Bravo!"

Not that I wasn't impressed with the designer, but come on, anybody can think up a shirt. It takes real talent to get all these women in one spot.

What is this goofy walk that all the models do? You know that walk? Down the runway, like they really have to go somewhere. You know how they're all wiggly, all full of importance and attitude. And then they get to the end and they look around and go, "Well, I guess I'll just go back."

I love to go to sports events. Love, love, love sports. Anybody running around in an outfit with a stripe on it, I want to watch them do it.

Take boxing, the simplest, stupidest sport of all. It's almost as if these two guys are just desperate to compete with each other, but they couldn't think of a sport. So they said, "Why don't we just pound each other for forty-five minutes? Maybe someone will come watch that."

It's strange, two guys in shorts competing for a belt. They should award them slacks or a shirt.

The real problem is that you have two guys fighting who have no prior argument. They should have the boxers come into the ring in little cars, drive around a little bit, eventually there's an accident. They get out. . . .

"Didn't you see my signal?"

"Look at that fender!"

Then you'd see a real fight.

My question about women's gymnastics is simple. Are we not supposed to be looking at their little rear ends while they're jumping around all over the place? Because I think that's pretty much all I've been doing, and I don't know if it's wrong. I mean if it's wrong, I'll stop, but no one's ever said anything about it. The announcer never goes, "In judging this event they throw out the high score, the low score, and stop staring at their little rear ends."

They really do have the most unbelievable rear ends in the world and it's hard not to notice it. Whenever they talk about what this girl needs to do to win I'm thinking, "Win? Win what? I think we have a winner right here."

You know how race-car drivers and tennis players get paid to have a company name sewn onto their uniform?

JERRY SEINFELD

Can you imagine how much money these women gymnasts could make if they sold advertising in the right spot on that little leotard? All it would have to say is DIET SLICE on one cheek and she's set for life. The greatest ad space ever. "We guarantee people will see your message. Your product will be a household name in the qualifying round."

Professional wrestling. The question you have to ask yourself about professional wrestling is also a simple one.

If professional wrestling did not exist, could you come up with this idea? Could you envision the popularity of huge men in tiny bathing suits pretending to fight? Could you sell this to a promoter?

"I'm telling you, Sid, millions of people will enjoy watching this. The guys'll be huge, we'll put them in little suits, and they won't really fight."

Professional wrestling is the only sport where participants are just thrown right out into the audience, and no one in the crowd thinks anything unusual is happening. If you're watching a golf tournament and Jack Nicklaus goes flying over your head—first of all, I would say you're watching a very competitive tournament.

And how about the professional wrestling referee? There's a great job. You're a referee in a sport with no rules of any kind. How do you screw that up?

The referee is kind of like Larry of the Three Stooges. You don't really need him, but it just wouldn't be the same without him. They must get these guys from the same place the Harlem Globetrotters get their refs. There must be this whole school where they teach you to just kind of run around and not notice anything.

They sit you down, show you a film of the rubout scene from *St. Valentine's Day Massacre,* and if you don't see anything illegal going on, you're hired.

The opposite of this is Olympic platform diving, where the judging is so critical, it's too depressing to even watch.

If the diver makes too big a splash going in the water, all the judges are like, "What the hell was that? That was the dive? Well, that's just no good at all. Too much splashing. I didn't like the splashing. A couple of drops almost got on me. He's just going to have to learn to slow down before he hits that water."

Don't these divers ever get frustrated and want to just do a cannonball? Wouldn't that be great to just see a wall of water going over the judges' table?

JERRY SEINFELD

They'd be wiping their glasses, "I didn't see the entry. What did you put down?"

Professional football. To me the hardest part of being a professional football player is on the one hand you're a millionaire on the other they blow a whistle and you have to run around after a football.

To me the whole idea of being a millionaire is somebody throws a football at me. Maybe I catch it, maybe I don't. I would think you get someone to hand you the football at that point.

"Here you go, sir, that's another touchdown for you. Would you like a fresh-squeezed orange juice before the next play?"

The movies will always be one of my top all-time out activities. But to be honest, the peak moment for me is always being on the way to the movies. I love being on the way to the movies.

We're in the car, trying to get there in time. Maybe you'll have good seats. Maybe it'll be a good movie. Maybe everything'll be good. You don't know, and when you're on the way it's still possible. I love that I'm definitely doing something and I haven't done it yet. That's a pure life moment. After you get a job and before you have to do it. Nothing beats that. It's the spaces between life that I like the most.

There definitely seems to be an age gap in the hiring policy at most movie theaters.

They never hire anyone between the ages of 15 and 80. So the girl that sells the tickets, she's 10. Then there's the guy that rips it, he's 102. So what happened in the middle there? They couldn't find anybody? It's like they want to show you how life comes full circle.

When you're 15, you're selling the tickets, then you leave. You go out, you have a family, kids, marriage, career, grandchildren. Eighty years later, you're back in the same theater, three feet away, ripping tickets.

Eighty years to move three feet.

My most embarrassing movie moment is how often I get confused by the plot.

I hate to have to admit it, but I'm one of those people you always see in the parking lot after the movie talking with his friends going, "Oh, you mean that was the same guy from the beginning? Ohhh." Nobody will explain anything to you while the movie's going on.

You can't find out.

I'm always whispering to the person next to me. "Why did they kill that guy? I don't understand. I thought he was with them. Wasn't he with them? Why would they kill him if he was with them? Oh, he wasn't really with them. Oh. . . . It's a good thing they killed him."

There's a lot of shushing going on in movie theaters. People are always shushing. "Shhh, shh, shh, shhh." It doesn't work because nobody knows where a shush is coming from. They just hear, "shh." "Was that a shush? I think somebody shushed me. I think I just got shushed, but I don't know where it came from."

Some people you can't shush in a movie theater. They're talking and talking, everyone around them is shushing them, and they won't shush. No one can shush them. They're the "unshushables."

The one movie ad I don't get is this one: "If you see only one movie this year . . ." If you see only one movie this year, why go at all? You're not going to enjoy it. There's too much pressure. You're sitting there, "All right, this is it for 51 more weekends, this better be good."

OUT ON THE STREET

I'm on the street the other day, I make a pay phone call, go overtime on the call, hang up the phone, walk away. You know what happens.

The phone rings.

It's the phone company—they want more money. Don't you love this? You've got them right where you want them for the first time in your life. You're on the street. They're on the phone. There's nothing they can do. I like to let it ring a few times, let them sweat it out a little, then pick it up:

"Yeah, hello operator hello? Yes, I'm here. . . . Oh, I've got the money. . . . I've got the money right here. Do you hear that? (tapping on receiver) . . . That's a quarter. . . . Yeah, you want that, don't you? Well, I didn't think the connection was that good. Plus, you interrupted me a couple of times. I didn't like that very much either. I'm going to think about this whole thing, why don't you call me back? I'll be in the general area—ring them all."

You know there's always one store location in your neighborhood that's constantly changing hands. Everybody has one of these in their neighborhood. It's a leather store, it's a yogurt shop, it's a pet supply. It's constantly changing. Nobody can do business there. It's like some sort of Bermuda Triangle of retail. Stores open up and then they just disappear without a trace. Nobody knows what happened to them. I guess eventually when aliens land from the mother ship like in *Close Encounters,* the bottom will slowly open and all these store owners will come wandering out in a daze going, "I thought there was going to be more walk-in traffic, didn't you? Nobody even looked in the windows."

Went to the zoo a few weeks ago. Went into the snake house. You know, why don't they just tell us the truth already? Just come out and say it. They're all dead. Why bother catching a live snake? It's much harder and it looks the same. And the alligator pit? They've got cigarette butts, pennies on their head. Wait'll the Gucci rep sees them. "All right the big one—luggage. The little fella, keycase and a wallet. Let's go, boys, you're in retail." They're in the front seat of the station wagon. "I told you we should've moved around."

Malls are so easy to find, but it's so hard to find anything *in* a mall.

They have the directory, but the problem with the directory is even if you figure out where you are, and where you want to go, you still don't really know which way to walk because it's an upright map. If you had like suction-cup feet that you could just "phhhp" walk right up on it, then you could tell. You could just be on it going, "All right, I'm here. I wanna go to the Gap, that's down there. All right, now I'll just walk that way." And people would know you. They would see you walking down the mall going, "It's one of those suction-cup guys. I heard about that guy. He's never lost."

Every mall has a Hoffritz in it. I'm sorry, but this has got to be kind of a scary place to work. They put like a 16-year-old girl behind the counter, and all day people are coming in saying things like, "I need knives. I need more knives. Do you have any bigger knives? Sharper knives? I need a big, long, sharp knife. That's what I'm in the market for. I like them really sharp. Do you have one with hooks and ridges on the blade? That's the kind of knife I'm looking for. I need one I can throw, and I need another one I can just hack away with. Do you have anything like that?"

The problem with the mall garage is that everything looks the same. They try to differentiate between levels. They put up different colors, different numbers, different letters. What they need to do is name the levels like, "Your mother's a whore." You would remember that. You would go, "I know where we're parked. We're in 'Your mother's a whore.'" And your friend would go, "No, we're not. We're in 'My father's an abusive alcoholic.'"

To me, the whole city of Los Angeles is a mall. It's temperature controlled, plenty of parking, you don't really like it but you can get whatever you need while you're there.

The thing about L.A. that kind of threw me was the smog alerts. They will sometimes actually recommend that people stay indoors during the smog alert. Now maybe I'm way off, but don't you think, I mean wouldn't you assume, that the air in the house pretty much comes from the air in the city where the house is? What do they think, we live in a jar with a couple of holes punched in the top?

It's very strange. Do you realize it is now possible for parents to say to their children, "All right kids! I want you in the house to get some fresh air. Summer vacation, everybody indoors!"

If we really stuck with the classic Greek priorities, a sound mind in a sound body, the only two places we'd ever go is to a library or a gym. What's amazing to me about the library is that here's a place where you can go in, you take out any book you want, they just give it to you and say, "Please just bring it back when you're done." It reminds me of this pathetic friend everybody had when they were a little kid that would let you borrow any of his stuff if you would just be his friend.

That's what the library is, it's a government-funded pathetic friend. That's why everybody kind of bullies the library, "Maybe I'll bring it back on time, maybe I'll bring it back late. What are you gonna do, charge me a nickel? Oooh, I'm so scared."

But the health clubs are a little too strict.

What's with the high level of security? The picture I.D.s, the security guards, people signing in and out . . . What is this, NORAD? I mean the people that *have* a membership go twice a year, who's breaking in? Is this a big problem, people stealing exercise? And what if they catch the person, what then? They run. That's aerobic, makes it even worse.

On my block, a lot of people walk their dogs and I always see them walking along with their little poop bags. This, to me, is the lowest activity in human life. Following a dog with a little scooper. Waiting for him to go so you can walk down the street with it in your bag. If aliens are watching this through telescopes, they're going to think the dogs are the leaders of the planet. If you see two life forms, one of them's making a poop, the other one's carrying it for him, who would you assume is in charge?

I say, if this is where we're at after 50,000 years of

civilization, let's just give up. I'm serious, let's pack it in. It's not worth it. Let's just say the human race as an idea didn't quite work. It seemed good at first, we worked on it for a long time, but it just didn't pan out. We went to the moon but still somehow wound up carrying little bags of dog doody around with us. We just got mixed up somewhere. Let's just give it over to the insects or whoever else is next in line.

IN

I painted my apartment again.

I've been living in this apartment for years and years and every time I paint it, it kind of gets me down. I look around and I think, "Well, it's a little bit smaller now." I realize it's just the thickness of the paint, but I'm aware of it. It just keeps coming in and coming in. Every time I paint it gets closer and closer and closer. I don't even know where the wall outlets are anymore. I can't even find them. There's too much paint. I just look for a lump with two slots in it. It looks like a pig is trying to push his nose through from the other side. That's where I plug in.

But I like my apartment. I like it neat and I like it

clean. Neat and clean. That's the way I want to live. My idea of the perfect living room would be the bridge on the *Starship Enterprise:* big chair, nice TV, remote control. That's why *Star Trek* really was the ultimate male fantasy. Hurtling through space in your living room, watching TV.

That's why all the aliens were always dropping in, because Kirk was the only one that had the big screen. Friday night, Klingon boxing. "Everyone on the bridge."

Yup, neat and clean. That's the way I like it. But I don't like cleaning. Clean, good. Cleaning, bad. You add the "ing" and it's a whole different thing. So, I've got to get a maid. But I don't really feel comfortable with the maid either because there's that guilt when you have someone cleaning your house. You're sitting there on the sofa, they go by with the vacuum cleaner. "I'm really sorry about this. I don't know why I left that stuff over there. It was a mistake. I dropped it. I just wasn't thinking."

That's why I could never be a maid. I wouldn't have a good attitude. If I was a maid at someone's house, I'd find them, wherever they were in the house. "Oh I suppose you couldn't do this. . . . No, no, don't get up, let *me* clean up your filth. . . . No, you couldn't dust, that's just too tough, isn't it? Don't even try to help me. You rest. Save your energy so you can turn this place back into a filthy, stinking hole when I leave."

I don't cook.

I do have a kitchen, I've been in it.

To me a kitchen is just a big room to hold a toaster. That's the way I think of my apartment. Bedroom. Living room. Toaster room.

Winter. I'll turn the dial thing up to make the toast darker.

Summer. I turn it down. With the sun and hot weather, I like it a little more on the light side. That's as into cuisine as I get.

My other big home-cooking concern is if I use too big a plate. Because then I'll have to wash unutilized plate area. I hate to wash a part of a plate that didn't have food on it. This is really just throwing your life away. I'm wetting it, soaping it up, rinsing, drying it. It didn't even do anything. These are the things that add up and later in life make you say, "Where did all the time go?"

I consider myself a master life efficiency expert. For example, when I'm making my bed and I tuck in one side of the sheet, I stay bent over as I walk to tuck in the other side. Why stand up and then bend again? It's a waste of life.

When I finish with my cereal, I put the bowl away with the spoon in it. Why go to a separate drawer to get a spoon every morning? I'm going to need it, leave it there. How often am I going to use that bowl and not need the spoon that goes with it? I'll worry about that situation when I'm faced with it.

I have no plants in my house. They won't live for me. Some of them don't even wait to die, they commit suicide. I once came home found one hanging from a macramé noose, the pot kicked out from underneath. The note said, "I hate you and your albums."

For a while, I had this thing in my apartment called a police lock. It was actually like a 4' long bar that set into the floor and braced against the door. The idea behind it is once the burglar breaks into your house, this gives him something to beat you with. So they don't waste time looking around for a bust of Beethoven or something.

You're done sooner, he's home earlier. It works out best for everybody.

I've always liked apartment living, but what do you do when a neighbor is making a lot of noise at three o'clock in the morning? Can you knock on someone's door and tell them to keep it down? I can't do that. It means altering your whole self image. What am I, Fred Mertz now? What's happening to me? Can I do this? Am I a "shusher"? I used to be a shushee.

One thing I love about living in New York is it's every different type of person piled one on top of the other. I am for open immigration, but that sign we have in the front of the Statue of Liberty, "Give us your tired, your poor, your huddled masses." Can't we just say, "Hey, the door's open. We'll take whoever you got." Do we have to specify "The wretched refuse?" Why not just say, "Give us the unhappy, the sad, the slow, the ugly, people that can't drive, people that have trouble merging, if they can't stay in their lane, if they don't signal, they can't parallel park, if they're sneezing, if they're stuffed up, if they have bad penmanship, don't return calls, if they have dandruff, food between their teeth, if they have bad credit, if they have no credit, missed a spot shaving. . . . In other words, any dysfunctional, defective slob that you can somehow cattle prod onto a wagon, send them over. We want them."

It's amazing to me that people will move thousands of miles away to another city, they think nothing of it. They get on a plane—boom—they're there. They live there now. "It's just a thousand miles, I'm living over here."

Pioneers took years to cross the country. Now people will move thousands of miles just for one season. I don't think any pioneers did that. "Yeah it took us a decade to get there, and we stayed for the summer. It was nice, they had a pool, the kids loved it. And then, we left about ten years ago and we just got back. We had a great summer, it took us twenty years, and now our lives are over."

THE RIDE OF YOUR LIFE

Life is truly a ride. We're all strapped in
and no one can stop it. When the doctor slaps your
behind, he's ripping your ticket and away you go. As you
make each passage from youth to adulthood to maturity,
sometimes you put your arms up and scream, sometimes
you just hang on to that bar in front of you. But the ride
is the thing. I think the most you can hope for at the end
of life is that your hair's messed, you're out of breath,
and you didn't throw up.

CYCLE ONE

Everyone gets excited about a baby. Except the baby. It's no fun being a baby.

They don't know they're going to grow. They're born, they look down, they think, "Well, this is it. This is the body I've got. Tiny hands, giant head, bad plumbing. Where am I going to find a tie three inches long?"

And at 6 months old they immediately put you in charge of complicated toys you have no idea how to operate.

I had a busy box. All these knobs, buttons, switches. I'm working away. I don't know it's not connected to anything. I'd make in my pants, everyone gets upset, I'd think, "I got this thing set way too high."

And every meal is a complete mystery. They sit you down, put the bib on you, you think, "All right, lobster."

And you don't get it.

I was not a good eater as a child. My mother used to try to disguise the food to get me to eat it.

It never worked.

"Look, Mom, I know it's liver. I don't know how you got it to look like Cocoa Puffs. . . ."

I hated those little snack-pack cereals. Still do. Don't like portion control.

And on the side they would explain how to cut along the perforated lines and pour the milk right into the box.

What was the point of this? Pretending your parents couldn't afford a bowl?

But I have to say I enjoy adulthood. I enjoy the fact that now, if I want a cookie, I have a cookie. Okay? I have three cookies or four cookies or eleven cookies if I want. What was the big deal with the cookies? "Not before dinner." "Not too many." "You've had enough." "Not now." Well, now I'm a grown-up, give me the cookies! Many times I will intentionally ruin my entire appetite. Beyond recognition. Then I call my mother up right after it to tell her. "Hello Mom? I just ruined my entire appetite. . . . Cookies."

So what if I ruin it? See, as adults we understand, even if you ruin an appetite, there's another appetite coming right behind it. I see no danger in running out of appetites.

I loved getting ice cream from the ice cream man. I'd stand in line in the back of the truck. I remember the menu of the different ice creams was right by the exhaust pipe. The motor was running. My parents would go berserk if they ever caught me smoking a cigarette, but they'd let me stand there and breathe exhaust fumes for 20 minutes.

If they did a study I think they'd find every time a kid gets a Dixie cup from an ice cream man it's the equivalent of smoking two packs of Luckies.

I was always amazed how the ice cream man could just reach his hand in that little door and pull out whatever you asked for. It was like a magic trick. I used to think there was a little midget in there in a sub-zero suit just handing stuff to him.

As a kid, the only thing I really cared about was candy. Candy is the only reason you want to live when you're a kid. Ages zero through ten, candy is your life, there's nothing else. Family, friends, school . . . they're only obstacles in the way of getting more candy. And you have your favorite candies that you love. Kids actually believe they can distinguish between 21 different versions of pure sugar.

Only a seven-year-old kid can actually taste the difference. When I was a kid, I could taste the difference between different color M&Ms. I thought they were different. For example, I thought the red was heartier, more of a main course M&M. And the light brown was a mellower, kind of after-dinner M.

The thing that impressed me the most about Jawbreakers was that they just went right ahead and named them Jawbreakers. You could tell they didn't even hesitate. They went, "You know, the only person that would want a candy to be this hard would be someone out to literally break their jaw. By God, that's what these are. They're Jawbreakers!"

The other product I put in this category of being right out there is 2000 Flushes. Just no bones about it. "2000 Flushes, buddy. Right here." You ever see the guy that sells this product on TV? You believe him. You look at him, you know this man has stood over a toilet and flushed it 2000 times. I can picture the dinner table at his house.

The family sitting around, his chair's empty, everyone just picks at their food, no appetite. In the background we hear a flush. "One thousand five hundred and seventy-four, still blue."

When you're in your thirties, it's very hard to make a new friend. Whatever the group is that you've got now, that's who you're going with.

You're not interviewing, you're not looking at any new people, you're not interested in seeing any applications. They don't know the places, they don't know the food, they don't know the activities. If I'm introduced to a friendly guy at a club or a gym, it's like, "Hey look, I'm sure you're a very nice person, you seem to have a lot of potential, we're just not hiring right now."

Of course when you're a kid, you can be friends with anybody. There were almost no qualifications. If someone's in front of my house now, that's my friend, they're my friend, that's it. "Are you a grown-up? No? Great, c'mon in! Let's jump up and down on my bed!" And if you have anything in common at all—"You like cherry soda? I like cherry soda. We'll be best friends!"

JERRY SEINFELD

I had a parakeet when I was a kid. That was the only pet that I really enjoyed. We used to let him out of his cage and he would fly around, crash into these huge mirrors my mother had put in. Have you ever heard of this interior design principle, that a mirror makes it seem like you have an entire other room? What kind of a jerk walks up to a mirror and goes, "Hey look, there's a whole other room in there. There's a guy in there that looks just like me."

But the parakeet would fall for this. I'd let him out of his cage, he'd fly around the room and, BANG! With his little head, right into the mirror. And they have no helmets, no protection when they fly. Just that straight back hair-do. Very aero. And I'd always think, "Even if he thinks the mirror is another room, why doesn't he at least try to avoid hitting the other parakeet?"

But you don't have to be that bright to qualify as a parakeet. It's a two-question test, "Can you fly? Is your head smooth? You're a parakeet."

I remember admiring my pets a lot as a kid. Because even if it was only a turtle, at least it was an adult turtle. I was still only a kid. I looked up to my turtle.

I really looked up to monkeys. Monkeys have contributed a lot to society in their way. They were the first astronauts in the Sixties. Which I'm sure made perfect sense in the monkey brain. "I see, so instead of the little bellhop uniform, you want me to get into a rocket and orbit the earth at supersonic speed. Yeah, I think that is the next logical step for me. Because, I been working with the Italian guy and the crank organ and I feel I'm ready to handle the maximum re-entry G-forces."

I think when you're a kid, you ponder life's mysteries a lot more. One thing I always wondered about is where are bugs going? Bugs never hang out. They're always on their way somewhere. You put your hand in front of them, no problem, they go someplace else. Whole new destination. I guess if you were walking along and someone dropped a 200-foot wall right in front of your face, you might go, "You know, I think I'll head to Toronto for a while. I don't need to live where there's giant walls falling out of the sky."

Bugs don't panic in these crisis situations. And when a bug's best friend is a 5-year-old boy, this is a crisis situation. He could put you in a jar with 2 blades of grass to live on for the rest of your life. He might find a magnifying glass on a sunny day, things happen.

Because in his mind, every 5-year-old kid is a mad scientist. He's got the white coat, the clipboard, the hair is out. You don't just capture bugs, you must test them. Test their endurance, their ability to withstand pain. Not for your own pleasure. For scientific reasons, of course.

I was a Cub Scout when I was 9 years old. All Cubs feel a certain bond no matter whatever else they may do in life. When you have had a little yellow button on the top of your head, you never forget. "Semper Cub."

I remember I'd get the outfit all set up: blue pants, blue shirt, little yellow handkerchief, the giant metal thing to hold the neckerchief together. Then I'd go outside, get beat up, come back, put my regular clothes on. You're not making it to school in that outfit. That's why we formed packs to survive. It's also why they taught us to camp in the wilderness. If we had normal clothes, we'd check into a hotel like everyone else. In that getup you want to be in the woods.

Actually, the only memory I have of being a Cub

Scout was trying to get my hat back. That was all I did. Run back and forth at my bus stop going "Quit it."

I think the first merit-badge book was *Wolf,* then *Bear.* I never got past *Bear.* I thought, "Wolf, bear, this is a pretty slow progression. At this rate we'll never get to women." I was thinking, "Come on—nightclubs, birth control, pick up the pace. I'm not meeting a lot of bears out there."

Gym class was another little brush with fascism. You line up in your squads, and you better be wearing your little gym suits. If you are not wearing the gym suit, you are not taking gym class. "Remember kids, exercise has no effect unless you're wearing these special suits."

A gym teacher is a strange occupational choice. What is this job? You're walking around in shorts with a whistle all day long. You've got an office next to a shower, you're torturing and humiliating young boys all day. It's weird. Always walking by the shower, it's like a porno movie.

Any day that you had gym was a weird school day. It started off kind of normal. You had English, Geometry, Social Studies, and then suddenly you're in *Lord of the Flies* for forty minutes. You're hanging from a rope, you have

JERRY SEINFELD

hardly any clothes on. Teachers are yelling at you, "Where's your jockstrap?!" Kids are throwing dodge balls at you, snapping towels—you're trying to survive. And then it's History, Science, Language.

There's something off in the whole flow of that day.

IQs, SATs, GREs, it's all initials. They don't even give you enough credit that you can understand the name of the test. That's your first confidence booster. Then there's the sample question at the beginning where they show you how to fill in the circle. This should be the first elimination point right there. Anybody goes outside that circle, "Yeah, you wanna come with us please, yeah, yeah, you're done, your test is over. You went outside the circle, there's no point in continuing."

I always did well on the essay questions. Just put everything you know on there, maybe you'll hit it. And then you'd get the paper back from the teacher, and she's just written one word across the entire page, "vague." I thought "vague" was kind of a vague thing to say. I'd write underneath it, "unclear," send it back. She'd return it to me, "ambiguous." I'd send it back to her, "cloudy." We're still corresponding to this day. Hazy, muddy . . .

One of the problems in life is that when you're a kid you have a certain way of working out disagreements, and those laws do not work in the adult world.

Kids could always resolve any dispute by calling it. One of them will say, "I got the front seat."

"I want the front seat."

"I called it."

And the other kid has no recourse. "He called it, what can I do?"

If there was a kid court of law it holds up. "Your Honor, my client did ask for the front seat."

The judge says, "Did he call it?"

"Well, no, he didn't call it. . . ."

He bangs the gavel.

"Objection overruled. He has to call it. Case closed."

Do you ever sneak down to better seats at the game, and get caught by the usher? When you're a kid, it doesn't matter because you're always getting chased from everyplace anyway. But when you're an adult, it's really embarrassing to get caught. You have to pretend like there's some confusion. So you put on this whole act, you're looking at the tickets, "I don't understand how this could've happened. Let me see . . . Oh I see the problem. These are very good seats, I have very bad seats. That's the misunderstanding."

When I was a kid, my favorite ride was the bumper cars. What a wonderful fantasy of the driving experience as it could be. All confrontation, no destination. That's what the bumper cars are. Driving as an act of pure hostility. But there was always one kid on the bumper cars that couldn't do it. As soon as the ride got started, he'd be stuck in a pack of empty cars, usually ending up with the attendant hanging off that big pole, helping him steer.

I always preferred a machine ride to anything live, like a pony ride. There's always a creepy guy that runs it. He's depressed, the pony's depressed. The whole thing's a big downer.

I've never really understood the pony. I remember being taken on a pony ride when I was a kid. And I'm not positive but I'm pretty sure I never actually asked for this.

It's a very slow, smelly, uneventful experience. It barely even deserves the term *ride*. It's a brain dead schlep through a dusty dirt and dung patch. I'm sitting on the thing, and the guy is leading it around a 20-foot circle. And even as a kid I remember thinking, "Oh, this is just too pointless. Someone get me off this freaky little mutant."

Why do we have these animals anyway? Besides the pony ride, what is the point of the pony? Police can't use them for crowd control. I assume that somehow somebody genetically engineered these horses to be this size. Could they make them any size? I mean, could they make them the size of a quarter if they wanted? That would be fun for Monopoly, wouldn't it? You put him on the board. . . . "Baltic, that's one more, fine, right there, hold it right there."

The best toy I ever had as a kid was when somebody got a new refrigerator and I got that big brown cardboard box to play with.

Because, as a kid, this is the closest you're going to come to having your own apartment. You can crawl in, "I'll live here from now on." Cut a hole for a window, stick your head out.

"Mom, Dad, you must come over some time. We live so close. I'm on the front lawn. It's the Frigidaire building, apartment #1."

PARENTAL INFLUENCE

When you're a kid, and you're in the back seat of your parents' car, it's like you're a prisoner back there. You're being held captive. There's nothing to do back there. All the good stuff's up in the front seat. You look up there, the steering wheel, the radio, the temperature controls, it's all up there.

"Ooh, if I could get my little hands on some of that stuff. I would be making some changes, boy. We would not be listening to this, I'll tell you that."

The one thing I loved about it is that you didn't have to sit in those child safety seats, so we could stand up in the back seat of the car. I remember being small enough to stand straight up back there. My head didn't even hit the ceiling. And we had that bench seat, you know, and you could lean on it like it was a bar. "So how fast you think we'll be going, Dad? Could I get a Cherry Coke here?"

My parents had two constant arguments while they were driving, over how fast my father was going or how much gas was left in the tank. My father had a standard defense for either one of these. It was always, "That's because you're looking at it from an angle. If you were over here, you'd see. From where you're sitting, it looks like I'm doing ninety on empty. But that's because you're over there. If you were over here, you'd know I'm in the driveway with a full tank."

Parents like to drag kids to these historical sites on vacation. I remember going to Colonial Williamsburg and you see these supposedly authentic blacksmiths there. You know, he's got the three-cornered hat, the knickers, the Def Leppard T-shirt. Later you'd see him pulling out of the parking lot in a Camaro. "Hey, Dad, isn't that the blacksmith?"

Do unemployed blacksmiths stand around talking about possible jobs, going, "Yeah, I got a few irons in the fire."

JERRY SEINFELD

My parents took me to the Amish country, which to a kid, to see a bunch of people that have no cars, no TV, no phone, you go, "So what? Neither do I." Who wants to see a whole community that's been grounded? That's the way they should punish the kids after they've seen Amish country. "All right son, get up to your room. That's it, I've had it, you are Amish, young man. For the rest of this weekend. Did you hear me? Amish! And don't come down till you've made some noodles and raised a barn."

All fathers are intimidating. They're intimidating because they are fathers. Once a man has children, for the rest of his life, his attitude is, "To hell with the world, I can make my own people. I'll eat whenever I want, I'll wear whatever I want, and I'll create whoever I want."

You don't ever really want to visualize your parents having sex. It's very uncomfortable.
You know in your mind that they had to have sex at least once to have you, but you still kind of maintain the image in your head, "Well, I don't know. I'm not positive. I can't prove it. I don't know if that actually happened." That's why I think if I found out I was adopted, that

would really come as great news. "I'm adopted? That's great." I'd be happy to hear that. That means technically, it's possible that my mother and my father are really just really great friends.

I mean sex is a great thing and all but you don't want to think that your whole life began because somebody maybe had a little too much wine with dinner.

You can't beat adult power. Unlimited television. Cake anytime you want. Plus, you can go home tonight and screw around with that thermostat all you like. We're in charge of it now.

My father got me so crazy with that thing. I didn't go near a thermostat until I was 28 years old. I was in a hotel room somewhere when I finally got up the guts to move it a little bit. The whole night I couldn't sleep. I was afraid my father was going to burst in the door, "Who touched the thermostat in here? You know I set it there for a reason." I waited years for my father to take me aside and explain to me the secret of the thermostat.

And then one day he did sit me down, told me this whole story about the sperm, the egg, intercourse. I said, "Dad, who cares? Get to the part where the thermostat comes in."

JERRY SEINFELD

I come from the kind of family where my mother kept an extra roll of toilet paper on the tank in back of the toilet, and it had a little knit hat with a pom-pom on it. I didn't know if the purpose of this was so people wouldn't know that we had an extra roll of toilet paper or because my mother felt even toilet paper is embarrassed to be what it is. The toilet paper had a hat, the dog had a sweater, and the couch arms and back had little fabric toupees to protect it. I never felt the need to try drugs growing up. My reality was already altered.

Parents make the best employers. Because no matter how bad a job you do they're stuck with you.

I used to mow the lawn for 5 bucks on the weekend. I was the worst. Sometimes I wouldn't even turn the mower on. I'd just make the lines with the wheels and say I was done. And there was nothing they could do. My father couldn't go, "Listen son, you're not really cutting the mustard out there on that lawn. Now I know you've been in the family for about 15 years, but I'm afraid we're going to have to let you go. Don't feel too bad about it. We're making cutbacks all over the house. The dog's only coming in 3 days a week."

My parents live in Florida now. They moved there last year. They didn't want to move to Florida, but, they're in their seventies and that's the law. You know how it works, they got the leisure police. They pull up in front of the old people's house with a golf cart, jump out. "Let's go, Pop. White belt, white pants, white shoes, get in the back. Drop the snow shovel right there. Drop it!"

And all my father would do down there is go in the hot tubs, the saunas, the Jacuzzis. And I'd have nothing to do, so I'd go with him. I'll tell you, you get into a hot tub with three or four really old men, this is not the cover of the Club Med brochure. They get out of that tub, it looks like an ad for gravity. "Look what gravity did for me. It can work for you too."

Is Florida not hot and muggy enough for these people? They love heat. If they ever decide to land men on the Sun, I think these old retired guys will be the only ones that will be able to handle it. They'll just sit there on the sun, on redwood benches, washcloths on the head, going, "Close the door! I'm trying to get a sweat going. You're letting all the heat off the sun."

JERRY SEINFELD

I have never seen an old person in a new bathing suit in my life.

I don't know where they get their bathing suits, but my father has bathing suits from other centuries. If I forget mine he always wants me to wear his. "You need trunks? Son, I got trunks for you. You can wear my trunks." Fathers don't wear bathing suits, they wear trunks. It's kind of the same thing a tree would wear if it went swimming. So I get in the water in this thing, and it's like floating around me somewhere. Did you ever put on a bathing suit that you don't even know exactly where you are inside the bathing suit? You see somebody you know, "No, I'm parasailing, I'm just waiting for the boat to come back."

I am not much for the family gathering. You ever sit there and the conversation's so boring, so dull, you start to fantasize, "What if I just got up and jumped out that window?" Just crashed right through it. Come back in, there's broken glass, everybody's all upset.

"No, no, I'm all right, I was just a little bored there, I'm fine now, I'm ready to hear a little more about that Hummel collection, Aunt Rose. Let's pick it up right there."

Aren't you a little surprised by the popularity of the camcorder? Especially with parents. Did we learn nothing from the home movies that our fathers took of us when we were little kids? I mean, just think back to your home movies, what do you remember? It was all just one endless shot of people going, "Get out of here, turn it off, get away, you're annoying everyone." There was no sound track back then. We thought they were just waving.

I can barely stay interested in my real life—live, in color, happening right in front of me. Why would I tape my life and then sit down to watch a tape of something I could barely tolerate when it was actually happening? People are always showing me their camcorders. "It's got a zoom lens." Yeah, that's great. So you can get right up close to the boredom. That's terrific.

HOMESTRETCH

Something happens when a man reaches a certain age that The News becomes the most important thing in his life. I remember when it happened to my father. I'd never see him actually leave to watch it. I would just hear the TV come on in the next room and I knew it was 11 o'clock. Wherever he was in the house he'd vaporize at 10:59 and reappear in front of the TV.

All fathers think one day they're going to get a call from the State Department. "Listen, we've completely lost track of the situation in the Middle East. You've been watching the news. What do you think we should do about it?"

I'm at the age now where the roles reverse with my parents. I go shopping with them it's like trying to organize little ducklings. They're wandering all over. Quack, quack, quack. I'm trying to keep them together. "Mom, Dad is about 3 blocks down you want me to go get him or are you going to catch up? Dad, wait. You don't need to look at those, they have them everywhere. QUACK, QUACK, QUACK, QUACK. All right now, get in a line. We're going to cross here when the light changes. QUACK. Okay, come on it's green, let's go, let's go. QUACK, QUACK, QUACK."

I refuse to go with them to shopping areas anymore. They want to go out with me, I take them to a little pond, let them paddle around, dry them off and bring them home.

To me, the thing about old people is that everything about them gets smaller. You know, their bodies get smaller, they move into smaller places, they sleep less time, they eat smaller meals . . . except the car. The older they get, the bigger their car gets. They're all driving these Detroit behemoths. I've never understood that. And old people have a way of backing out of the driveway. They don't turn from side to side. Their attitude is "I'm old and I'm coming back." "I've been around a while, now. You watch out for me, buddy. I survived, let's see you do it."

And then once they get out there, they drive so slowly. I would think the less time you have left in life, the faster you would want to go. I think old people should be allowed to drive their age. If you're eighty, do eighty. If you're a hundred, go a hundred.

They can't see where they're going anyway, let them have a little fun out there.

The life expectancy now is like 72 for men, and 75 or 6 or something for women. It's amazing to think that just a couple thousand years ago, life expectancy was thirty, which in our terms would be that you get your driver's

JERRY SEINFELD

license around five, get married at nine, divorced at fifteen, in your late teens, you move down to Florida. I guess that's how Spring Break got started.

And eventually people are saying things about you like, "You know it's amazing, he's twenty-eight but he's still very alert. His mind is so sharp, you would think you're talking to an eleven-year-old."

You know you're getting old when you get that one candle on the cake. It's like, "See if you can blow this out."

The other thing I'm not looking forward to is when they have to help you with the blow. You know those birthday parties when everyone gathers around behind the old person and blows with them? It's sad, because old people don't know that they're being helped. They think, "Hey look, I'm blowing all these candles out. And I'm just inhaling. I'm in good shape. I'm going to live a lot longer."

Of course we all try and save time. Cutting corners, little short cuts. But no matter how much time you save, at the end of your life, there's no extra time saved up.

You'll be going, "What do you mean there's no time? I

had a microwave oven, velcro sneakers, a clip-on tie. Where is that time?"

But there isn't any. Because when you waste time in life, they subtract it. Like if you saw *all* the Rocky movies, they deduct that.

So you've got to be careful. You can take the Concorde to Europe, but if they show *Meatballs 4* on the plane, you're right back where you started from.

To me, if life boils down to one significant thing, it's movement. To live is to keep moving. Unfortunately, this means that for the rest of our lives we're going to be looking for boxes.

When you're moving, your whole world is boxes. That's all you think about. "Boxes, where are there boxes?" You just wander down the street going in and out of stores, "Are there boxes here? Have you seen any boxes?" It's all you think about. You can't even talk to people, you can't concentrate. "Will you shut up? I'm looking for boxes!"

After a while, you become like a bloodhound on the scent. You walk into a store, "There's boxes here. Don't tell me you don't have boxes, dammit, I can smell 'em!" I become obsessed. "I love the smell of cardboard in the morning." You could be at a funeral, everyone's mourning, crying around you, you're looking at the casket. "That's a nice box. Does anybody know where that guy got that box? When he's done with it, you think I could get that? It's got some nice handles on it. My stereo would fit right in there."

I mean that's what death is, really, it's the last big move of your life. The hearse is like the van, the pallbearers are your close friends, the only ones you could really ask to help you with a big move like that. And the casket is that great, perfect box you've been looking for your whole life. The only problem is once you find it, you're in it.